CW01661901

Heating your Church

by

William Bordass

CIO PUBLISHING
Dean's Yard, London SW1P 3NZ

ISBN 0 7151 7543 2

Published 1984 for the Council for the Care of Churches by CIO Publishing

Printed in England by Tasprint Ltd.

FOREWORD

Wherever church folk foregather these days, be they clerical or lay, the subject of church heating is liable to generate a great deal of discussion – or dare one say 'hot air'! The high standards of heating many of us are now accustomed to in our homes and in our cars contrasts with the high cost of fuel and other financial pressures such as the diocesan quotas, make it very difficult for parishes to heat their church buildings adequately and acceptably. For these reasons the Council has been pressed for some time to produce an up-to-date edition of *Heating Your Church.*

There is no shortage of people claiming universal, easy and over-simplified solutions to problems of church heating, such as double-glazing, radiant heaters or systems using warm air. In fact, however, heating a church building is a complex business, involving special factors such as intermittent requirements, influx of people, and particular environmental care for works of art or musical instruments. Radiant heaters can look unsightly and increase dampness; warm air systems can be noisy and indiscriminate in their output; and double-glazing may not save much or cure the problem of down-draughts. One is tempted to find material for a sermon in the information that each member of a church congregation produces energy equivalent to that of a 100 watt light bulb and 50 grams of water vapour per hour, when sitting and listening, and more when singing vigorously or doing manual work. All this goes to show that church heating really can be a complicated affair, and we make no apology for issuing this fairly lengthy and technical document. To attempt to simplify it might merely be misleading. The booklet has a full and clear table of contents, and incumbents, churchwardens and parochial church council members should find it invaluable for discussions with architects, heating consultants and contractors, if they wish to improve their church heating systems. Here we have a comprehensive and definitive work written especially for churches, and we are most grateful to Dr Bordass for all the work he has put into providing this clear statement of the factors affecting an important subject.

Eric Evans, Archdeacon of Cheltenham
Chairman, Council for the Care of Churches.

ACKNOWLEDGEMENTS

General acknowledgements and thanks must go to Bill Allen, who introduced me to the subject of church heating, to Henry Goddard, the author of the previous edition, to my wife Elizabeth, who has had to stand by during a process which took far longer than intended, and to the Council for the Care of Churches, for the same reason.

More specifically I would like to thank those who have contributed ideas and commented on earlier drafts of the text, particularly Bill Allen, Henry Baker, Paul Bartlett, Keith Darby, John Eaden, Geoffrey Eyers, Alan Hildon, Peter Jay, Roy Newton, R. Paknoham, Adrian Steadman and Garry Thomson. I hope I have taken most of their comments on board. The responsibility for all remaining defects is entirely my own.

Finally, my thanks to Charles Statham, for drawing and re-drawing the illustrations, and to Morag Bocker and Helen Boby, for word processing and re-processing the text.

William Bordass
Robert Matthew, Johnson-Marshall and Partners
London
August 1983

CONTENTS

Page

ILLUSTRATIONS AND TABLES

FURTHER READING

Building Research Establishment. Digests 110 and 180 and British Standard 5250 *Condensation.*

Chartered Institution of Building Services. *CIBS Guide*, Section A, Current Version in 10 parts. *CIBS Energy Code*, Current Version.

Church of Scotland. *Make the Most of It-- A Practical Guide to Energy Conservation in Churches.* 1980.

Council for the Care of Churches. *The Care and Protection of Stained Glass and other windows in Churches. 1979.*

Department of Energy. Fuel Efficiency Booklet No. 7 *Degree Days.*

Faber, O., Kell, J.R. and Martin, P.L. *Heating and Air Conditioning of Buildings.* Architectural Press, 1979.

The Gas Council. *Notes for Guidance on the Installation of Flueless Gas Appliances for Church Heating.* Watson House Bulletin Statement, 1957.

International Institute for Conservation. *Conservation Within Historic Buildings.* Vienna Congress 1980.

Marsh, P. *Thermal Insulation and Condensation.* The Construction Press, 1979.

McIntyre, D.A. *Indoor Climate.* Applied Science Publishers, 1980.

National Building Studies. Research Paper No. 23 *Condensation in Sheeted Roofs.* HMSO, 1958.

Newton, R.G. *The Deterioration and Conservation of Painted Glass: A Critical Bibliography.* Oxford University Press, 1982.

Thomson, G. *The Museum Environment.* Butterworths, 1978.

INTRODUCTION

'The usual form of church... has four ceilings of three different heights, making it difficult to extract the air at the level of the roof. The clerestory windows chill the warm air as it rises, and send it down in a cold douche on the heads of the congregation.'

'An architect is instructed to prepare plans... Occasionally some too active member ventures to ask the architect if he has made any arrangements for ventilation. He always receives the reply that the subject has received the most careful attention and that when the building is finished it will be found perfect in that respect.... Eventually the congregation is split between those who prefer rheumatism and bronchitis with open windows or those who prefer asphyxia with the windows shut.'

'If economy is the principal object, a cheap hot air apparatus is ordered... If wiser councils prevail, hot water pipes are fixed, but as they are generally placed beneath the floor in channels...they become speedily covered by a coating of non-conducting dust, and there is generally an unpleasant smell... The building is too frequently used but once a week, and is therefore hastily warmed at the end of the week, an operation very imperfectly perfomed.'

E.H. JACOB
Notes on the Ventilation and Warming of Houses, Churches, Schools and Other Buildings (SPCK, 1894).

Many of the problems of church heating today are no different from those in 1894. Nor are some of the solutions. Nevertheless, there is a major change in emphasis even since the 1970 edition of this publication. North Sea gas has been fully developed, there has been the energy crisis, and sustained economic growth is no longer taken for granted. Economic pressures and rapid developments in electronics and controls have brought many new and more efficient products onto the market and have given some older ones a new lease of life. Many churches cannot afford to run their central heating effectively, but lose congregation if it is inadequate; they are therefore pressed to change to new systems which claim improved comfort and lower running costs. However, the correct choice is seldom easy.

Changes to heating systems, their operation, or insulation to reduce heat loss, are often made without proper consideration of their effect on the building and the things it contains. In the past, continuous heating often dried things out excessively; the effect on organs being notorious. Today, it is well-known that the inappropriate, but often inevitable, use of heating in housing may cause condensation and deterioration of the building. Similar things are also possible in churches and ill-considered alterations this year could lead to large repair bills some way into the future.

More efficient heating arrangements, more effectively designed and operated to keep people adequately comfortable at the required times, can cut running costs to a minimum. However, as a result, the church has less heat put into it than before, though on a more measured basis. Unless the correct steps are taken, it will usually be damper.

Church heating thus must not be considered in isolation: the whole system of heating and ventilation, building, contents, users and operations must be taken into account. There are no universal answers: for instance a system which has performed satisfactorily in a building with a slate roof might threaten the integrity of a lead roof in an otherwise similar building.

It is hoped that this publication will help to establish some principles which may be followed. It is very much a general guide, rather than one for the heating specialist. It is also orientated towards the problems of existing churches and other large spaces in intermittent use, although the needs of new and more continuously-occupied buildings are also touched upon.

At the start is a summary and overview, followed by technical sections in which the background and the arguments are developed in more detail. Unfortunately, little research has been done and experience in some areas is limited. Comments, case studies and monitored results are sought by the Council for the Care of Churches in order to allow the widest possible experience to be built into future editions.

1. SUMMARY

Background

A well-heated church is by-and-large a Victorian invention and a late twentieth century expectation. Prior to the re-invention of central heating (given that some Romans had it in the first place), churches were largely unheated, although the privileged few enjoyed a fire or stove which gave local radiant heat.

Over the past thirty years, the rapid growth in domestic central heating and warm cars has led many people to prepare themselves rather less well for the cold and to expect buildings to be warmer. Increases in fuel costs have so far done little to alter this trend, which hits many churches particularly badly owing to their large volumes, massive and poorly-insulated construction, and relatively low intensity of use.

Coal-fired boilers and stoves used to be difficult to light and slow to warm up, and so they were often fired at low level through the winter and stoked more vigorously when required. These days, heating is more controllable and often off altogether, letting buildings cool down further between occupancy times. However, to warm up a traditionally-constructed church properly will frequently take at least a day; the warming-up process is expensive and often uncomfortable owing to the air currents created in the process.

By modern standards, many church heating systems are inefficient and badly-controlled, particularly for the way the buildings are now used. Although a lot can be done to overcome the obvious deficiencies, the costs of heating the whole building adequately will often be too high. The question then becomes how to achieve the best comfort with the funds available, and without adverse effects on the building and its contents.

Thermal comfort (Chapter 2)

In a small room, air temperature is often a good enough indicator of thermal comfort. However, surface temperatures, air movement and radiation are almost equally important, and become more of a problem in large spaces such as churches and halls. We are all aware of the effects of a cold floor, of draughts, and that we feel warm in the sun on a cold day, but not as used to considering the design and operation of heating systems in relation to such physiological effects.

The result is that we often do the wrong things by not getting to the root of the problem: we heat the structure of a building in an attempt to make it comfortable for an hour or two; the air gets warm at high level rather than where the people are; and in an attempt to warm up the building fast we create draughts which nullify the benefit of the warmth. To stop heat escaping may not be the main problem: windows are sealed but the draughts remain as they were heating-induced downdraughts; an intermittently-used building is insulated with little effect on comfort or fuel costs as the problem was more one of system design and the building's thermal capacity than of heat loss to outside.

Looking after the building (Chapter 3)

Heating systems and the way in which they are operated affect buildings and their contents. The visual and structural effects of installation and the possible dangers of fire, leakage, explosion, fumes and staining are easily understood. Less obvious but often far-reaching in its ultimate repercussions is the effect on the humidity of the air and hence on the prevailing levels of moisture in the building's fabric and its contents. As temperature is to comfort, relative humidity is to preservation, and there is a major potential conflict between the needs of the church and its contents and the desire to reduce heating costs by the use of fast-responding heating systems. Moderate conditions are best: excessive dryness can cause organic materials to crack and crumble; dampness leads to rot and corrosion; and fluctuations cause condensation and dimensional changes.

For a long time, heating often caused excessive dryness and many people assume that heating automatically dries buildings out. However, this is only necessarily so when there is continuous heating and copious ventilation. These days, heating is less sustained, fewer heating appliances draw combustion air from within the church, and there is less emphasis on ventilation for health, buildings instead being sealed up to avoid draughts and heat loss. This makes dampness a growing problem which heating alone may not alleviate.

Temperatures and humidities need to be monitored particularly where there are items of historic importance, and action taken to keep relative humidity within a satisfactory range. This may require better control of ventilation as well as the heating, and dehumidification may be worth thinking about in intermittently-heated churches prone to dampness.

Fuel-choice (Chapter 4)

Fuel choice is often restricted by local availability and by the needs and requirements of the most appropriate and economic heating equipment.

Natural gas is a common choice as it is usually the cheapest (though not by as much as a few years ago) and the simplest of the fossil fuels to use.

Its particular advantages are exploited in a number of special purpose air, convector and radiant heaters.

Liquefied petroleum gas is more expensive but useful for portable equipment and where natural gas is not available. Solid fuel's price advantage seldom works out so well in all but the smallest and the largest systems, owing to the operating and servicing requirements. Fuel oil is normally only practical in the lighter grades and economic only where natural gas is not available.

Electricity is expensive at full rate, but where there is an adequate supply it can be appropriate for occasional and local heating, owing to high efficiency and good control. Wider use may be possible where off-peak evening and weekend tariffs are available.

Heat emitters (Chapter 5)

Heat emitters are often regarded as a necessary evil, their most desirable properties being cheapness and invisibility. Such criteria, however, may lead to a high running cost. The varying characteristics of different types of heater need to be well understood, and so they are discussed at some length. Well-selected and located radiant and forced warm air heaters may often give the best comfort with the lowest running costs. Natural convectors are widely used: these require care in design to avoid draughts and heating the vault instead of the choir. Portable heaters can be a fire risk while those without flues require careful attention to ventilation rates, humidity levels, and conservation of valuable parts of the building's structure and contents. Some types of heater can usefully improve comfort conditions in small parts of the church (e.g: for a baptism or a choir practice), while others may prove disappointing.

Central heating (Chapter 6)

It is all too easy to regard central heating as the ideal, but other alternatives may be more effective and cheaper to run, particularly in intermittently-used buildings. Nevertheless, central heating has its attractions, not least in keeping fuel-burning equipment out of the church proper. Systems need to be carefully controlled in order to avoid waste, particularly when parts of the heated area are used more intensively than the rest. Central heating is better suited for more continuously-used buildings, and underfloor and warm air systems may be considered for new projects and major refurbishments.

Many churches have elderly central heating systems which are ineffective and expensive to run. The choice is often between overhaul or complete replacement. Sadly, replacement will often bring better comfort with lower running costs, though sometimes the existing system may be retained for background heating during cold weather.

Automatic controls (Chapter 7)

Automatic controls are essential for the majority of systems to improve performance and avoid waste. With recent developments, particularly in electronics, major advances on traditional practice are now possible at low cost. Nevertheless, controls should be simple for the user: if they are too complicated they can easily be ignored. Accurate control of boilers and room temperatures with central heating is particularly important: a lot of energy can otherwise be wasted. Controls must also be correctly selected, connected and calibrated in the first place.

System selection and installation (Chapter 8)

The criteria for selecting a heating system will often include items affecting controls, running cost, options for future change and preservation of the building, in addition to the required temperature standards. It is impossible to give prescriptive solutions, and professional advice will often be necessary on the system itself and on installation to avoid direct and indirect damage to the building. Measurement of temperatures and relative humidities gives a valuable check on performance and on possible risks to the fabric and contents.

Getting the best out of systems (Chapter 9)

All heating systems require care and attention to operate satisfactorily, safely and economically, and arrangements should be made for this to happen. The fuel consumption should also be checked at regular intervals: it is much better to have advance warning than to be confronted by a large bill. Inappropriate design, installation and control features will often be identified and be worth rectifying. For intermittently-occupied churches, attention to the heating system and its controls will normally prove more cost-effective than improving the building's insulation.

Conclusions

We cannot draw prescriptive conclusions in this book as circumstances differ. The choice varies with the church and the way it is used. The two most common conditions are:

Occasional use, as in most parish churches, with services on some or all Sundays and at other times for weddings, choir practice etc.

Daily use, as in most cathedrals, multi-use buildings, and where there are a lot of tourists.

The heat storage capacity of the building is the main reason to differentiate between different use patterns. To heat the building's structure each time before it becomes comfortable is a heavy penalty in an occasionally-used building but less significant when the use is more sustained. Conversely, although large savings are claimed for heating systems which do not have to warm the structure first, the benefit is most dramatic in occasionally-used and light-weight buildings; with more frequent heating the structure will become warm however the heat is introduced.

Excluding capital cost, appearance, and installation requirements, the principal considerations in selection will be:

1. What parts of the building need to be heated and to what standard?
2. When operated in the manner intended, will the system achieve an acceptable level of comfort?
3. Will the system have a beneficial effect on the building and its contents, particularly in terms of moisture balance?
4. What are the likely running costs?
5. In an existing building, to what extent is it wise and economic to retain parts of the existing system?

In making a choice, one should visit similar churches with comparable installations and talk to those who actually use them and pay the bills. Where alterations have been recent, authentic 'before and after' comparisons of fuel cost, comfort, humidity and the condition of the building should be sought.

Occasional use

The space in many churches is occupied for a remarkably short time, and it is seldom practical to maintain central heating where heat is only needed on 50 or so days in the year and for only a few hours on each occasion. The most economic means of making an occasionally-used church comfortable is to heat the smallest area possible by means of radiant or warm air systems, or a combination of the two. Individual heaters often prove more cost-effective than central systems, particularly in smaller churches.

Radiant heating is often cheaper to run than air heating, for a given fuel. There are visual problems owing to the need for an unobstructed line of sight from heater to person. Gas and electricity are the most convenient fuels for radiant heaters. The gas-fired units are usually the more powerful and are most appropriate for whole-church heating; they also tend to heat the air and the structure more. Electric radiant heaters can often be more flexibly located and more precisely beamed and controlled, but fuel cost and limitations in supply capacity often restrict them to more localised applications.

Oil and gas are the most convenient fuels for warm air heating. Large industrial units are low in cost but they are often noisy and air distribution is poor. A number of smaller balanced flue gas convectors with low speed fans are often more satisfactory, provided flues through the wall are acceptable visually and structurally, and the church is not too wide.

It is unlikely that single technique of occasional heating will alone give good comfort in cold weather unless running hours are extended; either its heat output will be insufficient or the heat supplied at one position will be too fierce.Two methods applied together, or one with a low level of background heating, will often be more satisfactory.

If a large church is normally heated at weekends only for a small congregation, part (e.g: a side chapel) might be screened off for the winter. Local radiant heating is also possible but its secondary effect of raising air temperature will not be as great as in a small church and there will be more need for background heating in cold weather.

Since the advantage of both warm air and radiant systems is a rapid warm-up, the structure of an occasionally-heated building remains cold: the heating will not dry it out much and water vapour introduced by the occupants and by flueless heaters may make it damper. Good ventilation (natural or mechanical), or dehumidification is thus a necessary adjunct: some ventilation is automatic with flued burners which draw their combustion air from within the church. There is competition between the need for ventilation and for fuel economy, warm air systems being the more sensitive to air change rates. Intermittent warm air heating also tends to cause rapid excursions in the relative humidity of the air, which can be bad for organs and for insubstantial artifacts not protected within suitable storage cabinets.

Where the entire church needs to be heated at weekends, more heating methods can be satisfactory, but they should be arranged and controlled to minimise draughts and stratification, allowing the building to become comfortable before it is fully warmed. In new installations, the following methods may be technically satisfactory:

Overhead gas-fired radiant heating.

Conventional hot water central heating, preferably using either large radiant heating surfaces or fan convectors.

Carefully ducted gas or oil-fired air heating, with flues. Flueless gas fresh-air heaters may also be appropriate in some circumstances.

Unit natural or fan-assisted gas convectors may also be considered where balanced flue terminals are acceptable. The air emerging from natural convector units is normally quite hot and tends to stratify; they are therefore best suited to churches with low ceilings.

In the centre of a large church, individually-flued units cannot easily be accommodated; and stratification and downdraughts can be more severe. Central hot water systems then become more practical and economic to meet the diverse requirements. Floor heating may also be considered when major alterations are being carried out, but it is usually best for continuous background heating to say 12–13°C.

Daily use

For continuous heating or continuous background heating with boosts as necessary, the slower-responding systems may sometimes be appropriate, particularly floor-warming, coal-fired boilers and occasionally off-peak electric storage systems. An existing underpowered central heating system, (possibly with a smaller, more efficient boiler) might be retained as background for cold weather, with an independent supplementary air or radiant heating system for top-up and sole use in mild weather. Heating with a good radiant component is generally preferable as, for a given fuel, the lowest air temperature consistent with the required comfort standard often gives the lowest running costs.

To simplify control, it helps to restrict the central heating systems only to the areas requiring full daily heating and for background heating elsewhere, and to deal with more occasional requirements in other ways: this reduces the potential for waste that can arise either from heating unnecessarily or from operating a large system inefficiently to meet a few localised heating requirements.

2. HEATING AND COMFORT

There are two main reasons for heating: to make people comfortable and to help look after the building and its contents. Heating systems should be designed to achieve these objectives effectively and economically.

In this chapter we discuss heating requirements, the criteria for thermal comfort, and how they may be met through planning, system design and operation, and avoiding draughts. In Chapter 3, we then look at the effects of heating on fabric and contents of the building, and the moisture content of the air.

2.1. Thermal Comfort

People do not in themselves need heating. The body produces heat by chemically burning up food. The rate depends on physical activity: about 70 watts when asleep, about 100 watts (equivalent to a light bulb) when sitting and listening, perhaps 150 watts when singing vigorously, and much more during heavy manual work. An individual is comfortable when the balance between this and the heat loss to the surroundings is reasonable.

The mechanisms of heat transfer between a person and his surroundings are the normal ones of convection, conduction, radiation and evaporation (figure 2.1). In a church:

> Convection is normally the most important and is a loss from the body, air even in warm buildings being cooler than the skin. The rate of heat loss is greater if the air is moving, owing to increased convection and evaporation. Losses from exposed parts of the body: hands, face, neck and ankles, are particularly important. The sensitivity varies: a refreshing breeze on the face can become an icy draught if it falls on the back of the neck. Cold draughts near the floor and women's fashions often cause discomfort in conditions which would otherwise be satisfactory.
>
> Heat transfer by conduction is generally quite small, and normally a loss: contact with surfaces any warmer than the skin becomes uncomfortable after a while. However, feet often get cold in a church, owing to the cold floor and to draughts at ankle level, and this has a disproportionate influence on perceived comfort. Carpets and cushions give limited, but useful, insulation and pew or underfloor heating can counteract the effect. When box pews are taken out, the loss of the wooden insulating floor and the barriers to air currents can often lead to complaints about the heating.

FIG. 2.1. HEAT TRANSFER AFFECTING THERMAL COMFORT

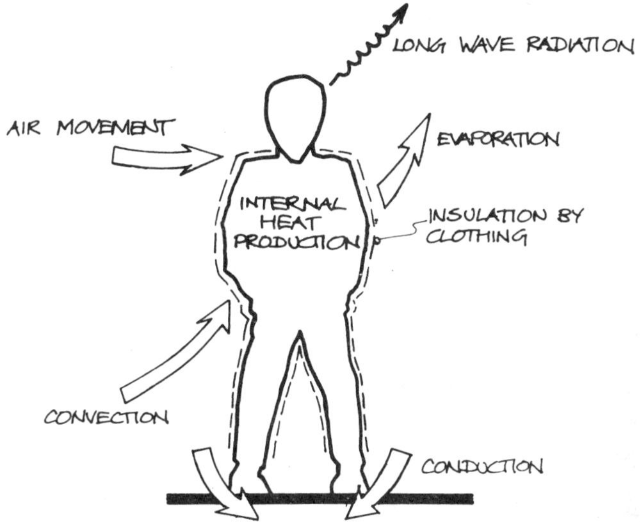

FIG. 2.2. RADIATIVE HEAT TRANSFER

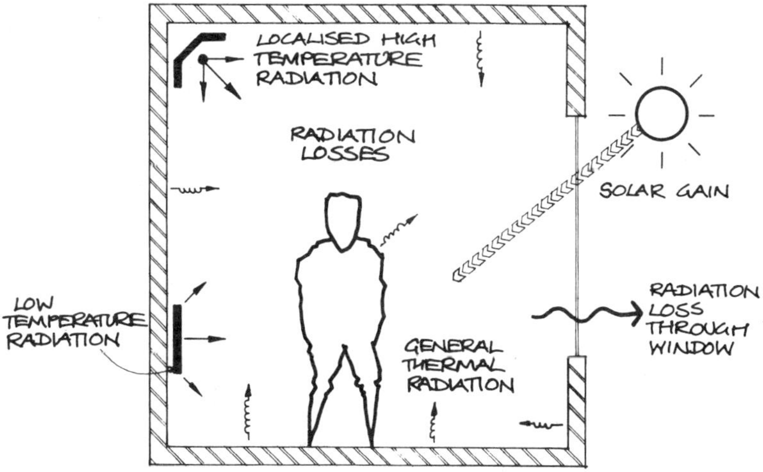

The effect of radiation on comfort is often overlooked. In normal clothing, radiation and convection are equally important, the radiant proportion falling a little as clothing becomes heavier. The heat exchange process is outlined in figure 2.2. The radiation from any surface is proportional to its area and increases very rapidly with its temperature. Small, high temperature radiant heaters are intense and clearly identifiable. Low temperature sources, such as the internal surfaces of a building, are also important owing to their large surface areas. A person surrounded by cold surfaces (at whatever distance) will feel cooler than if they were at room temperature, as he will be receiving less radiation from his surroundings. Conversely, if the surfaces are warm, the person will feel comfortable at a lower air temperature. Radiant heaters can thus be used to improve comfort when the air is cold, as the sun does on a frosty day. They have an important role in keeping people comfortable directly, without the need to heat the building or the air first, and without incidentally causing bad draughts.

Evaporative heat losses occur from the skin and particularly through breathing and singing, but their influence on comfort during the heating season is usually negligible. The moisture balance is, however, crucial for the building and its contents.

The variety of heat exchange mechanisms make air temperature a poor index of thermal comfort unless there is little air movement and air and surface temperatures are uniform and similar. The UK Chartered Institution of Building Services (CIBS) makes its recommendations in terms of 'dry resultant temperature', which in still air is the average of the air and radiant temperatures. Other factors affecting comfort are summarised in figure 2.3.

The CIBS recommended design value for dry resultant temperature in churches is 18°C (65°F), but for people in outdoor clothing and stockings 15°C, (59°F) is perhaps more realistic. Figure 2.4 shows how this may be obtained with a range of radiant and air temperatures. During cold weather, the temperatures of internal surfaces will be low, particularly if the church is heated intermittently, a mean radiant temperature of 10°C or less would not be uncommon. A resultant temperature of 15°C would thus require an air temperature of 20°C or more, or alternatively some radiant heating.

2.2. Absorption and Loss of Heat by the Building

The most straightforward means of achieving a comfortable environment is to heat the building thoroughly, and to control the air

FIG. 2.3. POSSIBLE SOURCES OF THERMAL DISCOMFORT

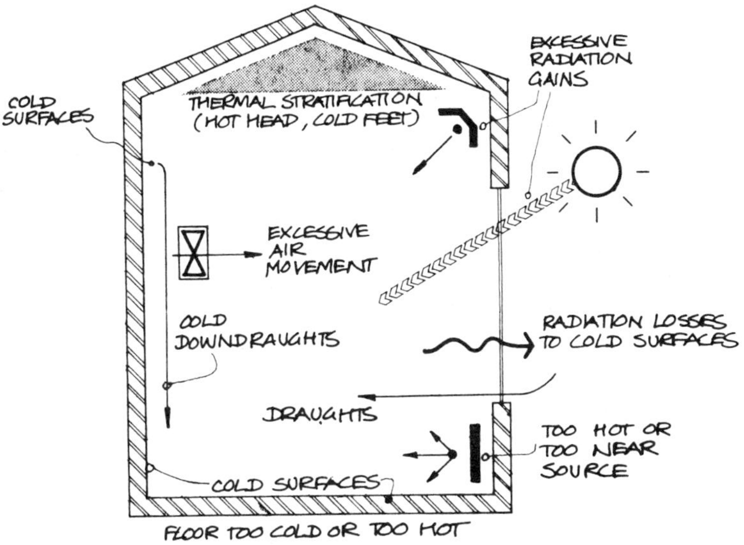

FIG. 2.4. RESULT OF DIFFERENT RADIANT & AIR TEMPERATURES

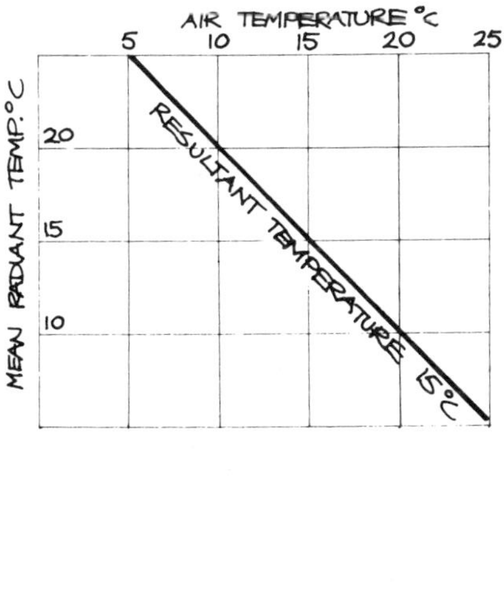

FIG. 2.5. EFFECT OF AIR VELOCITY ON RESULTANT TEMPERATURE

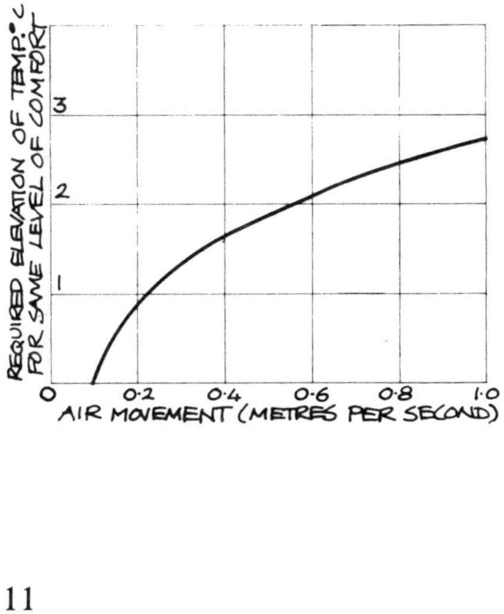

temperature using a detector at low level, where the people are. All internal surfaces are then warmed up, making radiant conditions reasonably satisfactory and avoiding the worst effects of conduction losses.

The rate of heat loss through a building element is known as the U-value (measured in watts per square metre of surface area per degree C of temperature difference between inside and outside). In traditionally-constructed churches, the heat losses will often be in this order of diminishing importance: roof, walls, windows, air infiltration, floors; totalling typically 1 watt per cubic metre of church per degree C of temperature difference between inside and outside. For small churches, which have a greater enclosing surface area and more air infiltration in relation to their volume, losses may be greater.

The Design Heat Loss is the rate of heat input necessary to maintain the required internal design temperature under specified external conditions (in the UK often −1°C, with no sun and under average wind conditions for the site). Calculation procedures are dealt with in standard works, such as the CIBS Guide (see bibliography).

With intermittent heating, additional heat output is necessary to warm up the structure and contents of the building and to counteract their 'cold' radiant effect. Heat sinks into solid materials at about 30mm per hour, and so it will take half a day or more to heat up most masonry walls. To heat up the building properly often takes longer, unless the system is substantially oversized. The thermal capacity has more effect than the insulation on warm-up characteristics, since insulation does not become fully effective until a steady state is achieved. Improving the insulation of massive elements in intermittently and occasionally-heated churches is thus unlikely to give the running cost savings which might be predicted from steady state calculations.

To heat a large church fully is expensive since a large volume of air and massive building elements need to be warmed. When systems designed for continuous heating are operated intermittently or occasionally, the result is often poor in relation to its cost because:

A greater proportion of the heat is used in warming up the system and the building.

With convective heating in particular, the building warms up at high level long before there is much effect lower down.

If the system has been sized for continuous operation, warm-up may take a very long time.

During the warm-up period, draughts are often created which can offset much of the benefit of the warmer air.

2.3. The Origin and Control of Draughts

Air movement at room temperature is noticeable if it exceeds about 0.15 metres per second (30 feet per minute), and can be unpleasant at twice this speed. Colder air is perceptible at lower speeds. Figure 2.5 shows the increase in air temperature required to counteract the cooling effect of air velocity. Where there are troublesome draughts, it is usually more cost-effective to tackle them directly, instead of increasing heating generally.

Draughts are normally ascribed to openings such as unlobbied entrances, badly-fitting windows, and unfilled eaves. However the mechanisms of heat supply and heat loss are often more important, particularly where heating is by convection. Common mechanisms are outlined below (figure 2.6):

> Strong descending convection currents (downdraughts) set up by air being cooled and increasing in density. These normally originate at windows; they also occur against the cold structure during warm-up.
>
> Strong ascending convection currents from natural convectors and stoves, which often set up a pattern of air circulation which includes downdraughts and cold air flowing across the floor.

Poorly designed, adjusted, or operated warm air and fan convector systems may also give air velocities too high for the temperature of the air discharged, or near return air inlets.

Heating-related draughts may be reduced by effective system operation. For instance, an obvious reaction to cold draughts in the better-warmed part of a church would be to turn up the heat locally. However, this may just accelerate the troublesome air circulation from the colder part to the warmer. It may prove more effective instead to operate the heating for longer at a reduced output, or to reduce the variation in air temperature and provide supplementary radiant heat where required.

Draughts from doors can be of local or psychological significance. A draught lobby is usually desirable, but it needs to be large (otherwise both doors are opened simultaneously) and of good quality; this often makes it too expensive. Instead, good closers and draught seals may be fitted (not inhibiting the operation of the door), with a curtain or screen to deflect air currents.

Draughts are difficult to identify correctly by 'feel' and smoke tests should be done if there are problems. It is revealing to observe the velocity and circulation of the currents, particularly near tall windows and convector heaters. An air current can 'stick' to a surface in a film very different in temperature to the adjacent air. A downdraught current may thus detach itself from a window cill, continue over the wall surface below, and travel across the floor. These air currents can sometimes be dispersed by introducing turbulence, which can improve local comfort substantially.

Unpleasant downdraughts from glass surfaces and the associated 'cold' radiant effects may also be counteracted by carefully-designed forced warm air systems or by a convector heater at their foot. With tall windows, it may not be possible entirely to neutralise the downdraught, but the cold air may be tempered or deflected out of harm's way (figure 2.7). Double glazing also reduces downdraughts and radiation loss, but is no panacea, particularly for tall windows.

In a large church with a triforium, cold air from the vault and clerestory may also fall onto the necks of the congregation. Heat may be introduced by:

- Pipes or compact natural convectors beneath the windows. Connecting pipework can be difficult to route satisfactorily.
- Electric tubular heaters fixed to the cills.
- Fan convectors or warm air outlets at floor level, as a last resort.

For smaller clerestory windows, deflectors at cill level may help mix the cool downdraughts with warmer air rising from the body of the church. The usefulness and the optimal design of the deflectors is best determined by experiment.

2.4. Heating for Comfort

Where a church is regularly used, it may be reasonable enough to achieve comfort by heating the building generally and avoiding stratification and draughts. In an occasionally-used building, this will be too expensive and it will be better to aim to achieve comfort more directly, and first:

- Encouraging the congregation to wear warm clothing, with particular emphasis on protecting their necks and ankles.
- Providing insulating floor and seat coverings.
- Avoiding draughts, particularly round the feet.

A suitable environment in terms of convection, conduction and radiation may often require more than one type of heating. Unfortunately, this often puts people off owing to fears of complexity and increased costs.

FIG. 2.6. COMMON ORIGINS OF DRAUGHTS

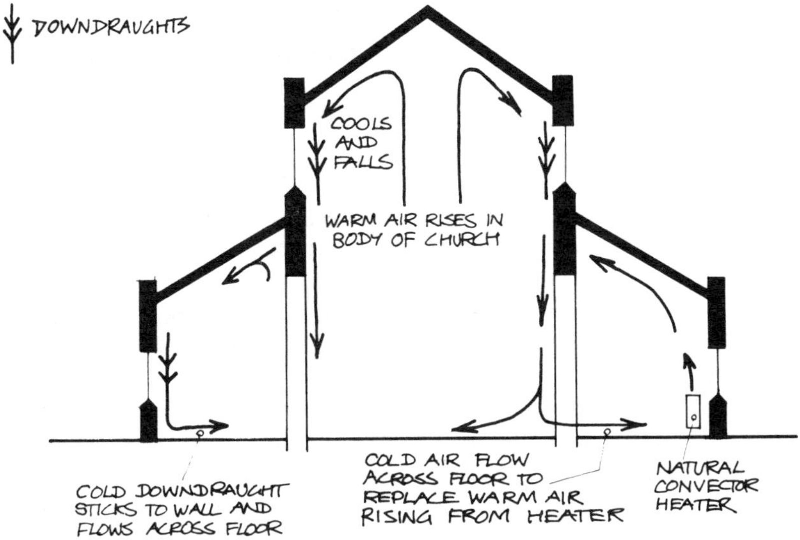

FIG. 2.7. CONTROLLING DOWNDRAUGHTS FROM WINDOWS

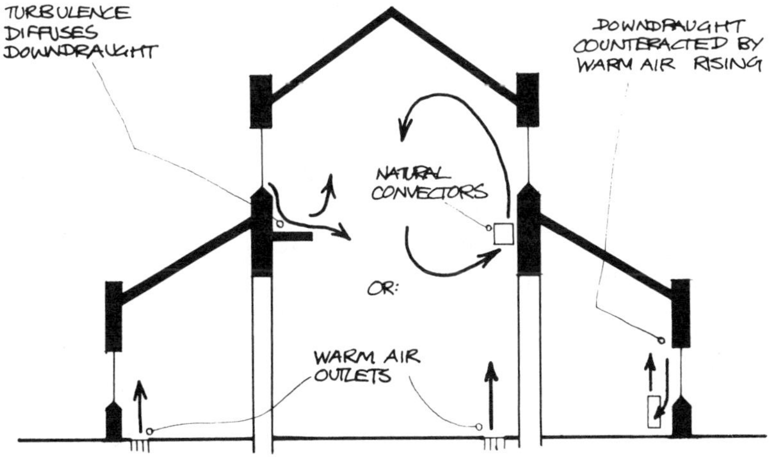

Heating for comfort only needs to be effective in occupied areas at the times of occupation. For instance, heaters to counteract cold downdraughts from windows need operate only during cold spells, at occupancy times and for a short preheat period.

An unheated building will have a cold floor, cold seats and low radiant and air temperatures. However, it need not be draughty as there will be few thermal convection currents. The following options can improve comfort at relatively low cost:

Pew or local floor heating (Section 5.5). This is not normally 100% effective but can provide a worthwhile improvement in local air and radiant temperatures and also avoid cold feet.

Warm air heating: large industrial blowers are popular but they can be noisy, give poor air distribution, and make the building feel both stuffy and cold owing to high air and low radiant temperatures. More sophisticated designs allow better control of air distribution: 'washing' surfaces with a warm air stream can help increase surface temperatures (and hence radiant conditions) without warming the building right through.

Radiant heating is often best in theory as it can be localised to the areas where the people are and also heats the floor and the seats. However, air temperatures should not be allowed to get too low (10°C is a reasonable minimum) and the systems have to be very carefully selected and designed to be effective. Unless fully embedded, radiant heaters tend to be conspicuous because there needs to be a line of sight between them and the people. A delicate balance therefore has to be struck between appearance and effectiveness.

Perhaps the best combination is local radiant heating with a low level of background heating to stop the building and the air becoming excessively cold; this also has advantages for the building itself, as discussed in the next chapter.

The sizing of an occasional heating system has little to do with design heat loss and preheat times: it depends more on the precise building and system characteristics and the comfort requirements. Advice should always be sought from designers and manufacturers: it is dangerous to assume that an installation which works well in one church will necessarily achieve similar results in another. For instance, the effects on performance of the seating and of the floor covering can be significant.

3. EFFECTS ON THE BUILDING AND CONTENTS

Heating is normally regarded as good for buildings, although heating systems are also known to cause specific types of deterioration. Indeed, some European authorities have concluded that no heating is best. In the British climate a little heating will normally be preferable, with suitable ventilation or dehumidification to avoid relative humidities becoming too high.

While buildings and the contents tend to do best with a gentle stability of heating, the most economic methods of heating for comfort tend to cause rapid variations in temperatures and humidities. Whether this causes problems for the building and its contents depends very much on the individual situation.

The temperate oceanic climate of the British Isles is unusual. The warm ocean currents which help heat the air also fill it with water vapour, resulting in high atmospheric humidities (particularly in the west) and consistent rainfall in all seasons. Most countries with similar relative humidity are tropical, most with our length of heating season are colder and drier and require heating more continuously. This makes the balance between heating, ventilation and humidity in buildings more critical in the British Isles than in most other parts of the world.

3.1. Consequential Effects of Heating on the Building

1. *Fire* Many fire risks are readily apparent and are minimised by compliance with regulations and codes of practice. The most common causes are faulty electrical installations and where boilers are altered without due regard for the construction and capacity of an existing flue or chimney. Portable heaters, except perhaps electric radiators with a low surface temperature and well protected elements, should always be placed on a non-combustible floor or surface and well clear of combustible materials, but fixed equipment is always preferable.

2. *Fumes* In a poorly-maintained system, combustion products may escape causing a safety and health hazard which should be corrected immediately. However, some gas and paraffin heaters are designed to discharge their combustion products into the heated space. The equipment is intended for use with good ventilation, otherwise water vapour, a major combustion product, can condense and may also accelerate attack, which is occasionally exacerbated by trace chemicals also present. This type of heater should not be used where the church is constructed of or contains potentially vulnerable items, as discussed in Section 5.4.

3. *Staining* Streaks above radiators, convectors, pipe brackets and warm air grilles are well known, as is pattern staining on ceilings. Their avoidance is discussed in Section 8.4. Leakage of liquid fuel may also cause staining and damage, and it is best kept out of the church proper.

Less obvious but often equally important are the effects of the design and operation of heating systems on moisture levels within the church, which can result in excessive dryness, condensation and dampness, or occasionally fluctuations between the two.

4. *Condensation and Dampness* The relationship between heating, humidity and the health of the church and its contents is so important that it is considered in detail later. In recent years problems of condensation and dampness in churches have increased, sometimes following changes in use and heating systems, and with a general trend to less ventilation and reduced hours of heating.

5. *Drying-out* Early central heating systems had a reputation for making buildings dry: dampness would disappear but natural materials, such as timbers and organ components, would shrink and crack. On occasions, new heating systems accelerated timber decay and insect attack where there were faults already, since temperatures and humidities became more sympathetic to the biological process. Heating also increases the rate of evaporation of moisture from rising damp, leaks and defective flashings. Although this helps clear the water from the point of entry, rot and insect attack may be accelerated: heating should thus never be used as a substitute for good maintenance and prompt repairs. Underfloor heating may drive moisture up adjacent walls and columns, and it is best to terminate the heated area 1 metre away from them. Accelerated evaporation of rising damp permits more water to rise into the building, bringing with it dissolved salts from the ground which may cause damage and efflorescence, and wall paintings are known to have been destroyed by this mechanism. Water evaporated from damp parts of the building may subsequently condense on cold surfaces or within materials which were previously dry, leading to further difficulties.

3.2. Additional Effects on the Contents

Valuable works of art, furnishings and records in a church need a suitable environment, preferably at a stable temperature, around 55% relative humidity (see below), and protected from chemical contaminants and dust. Specific requirements are a matter for the conservator. Ideal conditions will not normally be practical, but extremes should be avoided. For instance:

> Thin artifacts respond rapidly to changes in temperature and relative humidity and are prone to rapid deterioration where heating is intermittent and violent. Authorities recommend a rate of temperature change no greater than 1.5°C per hour.
>
> Pictures insulate, causing a lower temperature and a higher relative humidity between them and an outside wall. Free circulation of air behind should be arranged and a gap of 150mm (6 inches) is recommended.
>
> Where there is stratification, items high on the wall can get quite hot while the relative humidity of the adjacent air is reduced.
>
> Heat emitters and air grilles can place nearby items under thermal stress, be it from radiation, warm air, or merely rapid air movement. Staining must also be avoided.
>
> At high relative humidities, damage by chemical pollutants from industrial atmospheres and flueless heaters may be accelerated.

Many of the problems may be alleviated if the items are appropriately protected, for instance stored in cabinets with a degree of heat and moisture storage capacity, which 'buffer' the item from the changing external environment. The Parochial Records Storage Cupboard is one example. The organ has traditionally been an early victim of unsatisfactory humidities and advice should be sought from a specialist if major changes to the heating system or its operation are contemplated. Heat sources should always be kept away from the organ itself and any hot pipes or ducts nearby should be well insulated.

3.3. Humidity in the Air

Atmospheric air always contains moisture in the form of water vapour. The maximum carrying capacity (saturation humidity) depends on the temperature and is shown in the psychrometric curve (figure 3.1). For example, at 4°C air is saturated by about 0.6% of water vapour by weight, while at 14°C it can carry over twice and at 20°C three times that amount.

Most materials have a volatile moisture content which they exchange with that of the air, from a minimum when the air is completely dry to a maximum when it is saturated. The equilibrium content accords not to the absolute humidity of the air, but to its 'Relative Humidity' (RH): the percentage of the saturation amount at the given temperature. Figure 3.2 illustrates average daily and seasonal relative humidities of the outside air.

Relative humidities of 70% or more promote condensation, mould growth, and other corrosion and decay processes. Low relative humidities cause organic materials to shrink and become brittle. Since organic materials swell with rising RH and shrink as it falls, fluctuations can cause splitting and make applied materials, such as paints and glues, come away. When the RH fluctuates rapidly, the surface changes its water content and dimensions more rapidly than the underlying material, causing warping and further cracking.

A gentle stability is preferable, ideally in the RH range of 45–65%. Practically, 40–70% will usually be acceptable, except where there are specific preservation problems. Sustained RHs above 80% are to be avoided as they lead to moisture contents of 20% or more in timber and other organic materials, putting them at risk of fungal attack.

3.4. Condensation

When warm air comes into contact with cooler air or a cold surface, the RH rises, reaching 100% at the so-called Dew Point Temperature (figure 3.3), when condensation starts. This may be:

as a fog of small water droplets (as when we breathe out on a cold day),

as a surface film (as when we breathe on a mirror), or

interstitial, in the body of a material (as when we breathe through a scarf).

Surface condensation is obvious on harder, impervious surfaces, in particular glass, tiles and gloss paint. This can be relatively harmless, provided it drains away safely, though stained glass may be attacked. The damage to glass may be greater when condensation is modest as this allows chemicals to accumulate; copious condensation washes them off. Windows can be protected by secondary glazing, preferably on the outside with the interspace ventilated to the outside air. Window condensation can be a good warning of the need to ventilate and helps to remove excess moisture; where double glazing is installed moisture may instead accumulate elsewhere.

FIG. 3.1. THE PSYCHROMETRIC CURVE

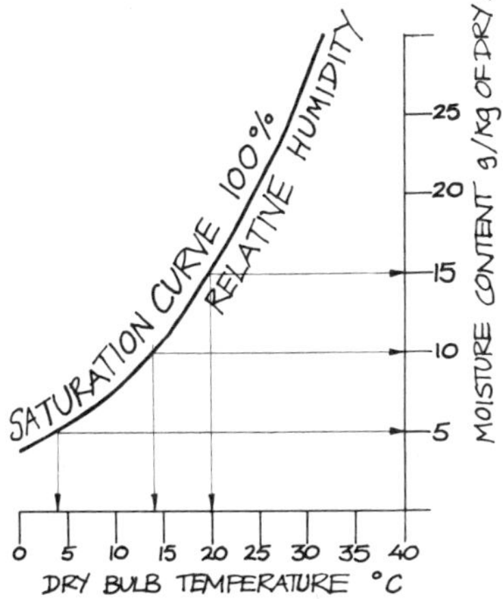

FIG. 3.2. TYPICAL ATMOSPHERIC HUMIDITIES

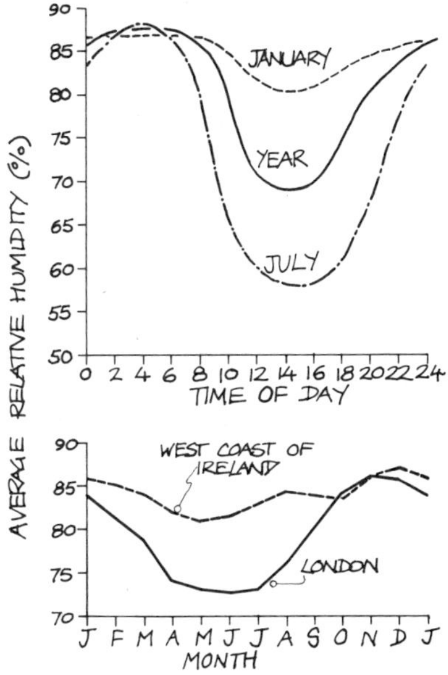

Water vapour will often diffuse readily through porous building materials and disperse harmlessly to the atmosphere. However, in a heated building, the temperature decreases towards the outside, possibly dropping below dew point if the porosity of the outer layers to water vapour is less than the inner ones (figure 3.4). Interstitial condensation then occurs; this may then reduce the insulating qualities of the materials, leading to increased heat loss and further condensation. Unfortunately, the dampness may persist for a long time before it or its effects are noticed.

Interstitial condensation most frequently occurs where insulation is used incorrectly. For instance, fibrous insulation applied internally may have little resistance to water vapour, but often lowers the temperature of the wall behind to less than dew point, allowing moisture to accumulate. A similar effect may occur where foam-backed carpet is laid over solid floors; this has caused brasses to corrode. Insulation over a ceiling may have little effect on water vapour transmission, but can reduce the mean temperature in the roof space to a level where the air change rate formerly sufficient no longer has the capacity to remove the excess water vapour. The air change may indeed have been reduced, deliberately or inadvertently, by blocking openings at eaves etc. when the insulation was applied.

Occasionally-heated buildings are particularly prone to condensation. Fast-reacting heating systems give an impression of warmth but the fabric remains cold. While the heating operates, water vapour enters the air rapidly by evaporation from damp materials, from the congregation, and especially from flueless heaters. When air heating is used, the moisture carrying capacity of the warm air may be sufficient to keep the RH at a reasonable level while the heating operates, although some condensation may occur in places. However, when the heating goes off, air temperature may fall rapidly, giving a high RH, possibly saturation. Rapid swings in temperature and humidity are also likely to cause articles within the church to deteriorate prematurely.

It is difficult to avoid condensation under all conditions and occasional accumulations frequently vanish harmlessly. For instance, water droplets are often seen under slate roofs after cool clear nights but usually disperse when it warms up the next day. With a metal-clad roof, however, dispersion is more difficult and careful attention must be paid to construction and ventilation details if problems are to be avoided. In recent years there have been a number of corrosion failures to the underside of lead sheet roofs as a result of entrapped condensation. The problem occurs most often following changes to heating, often with related decreases in ventilation; or a change in use, especially tourism, which introduces more moisture from people and catering facilities. In lead-roofed churches, consequential effects of change therefore need careful review. Advice is available from the Lead Development Association and the Ecclesiastical Architects' and Surveyors' Association.

3.5. Humidity Levels Inside Churches

The first influence on the relative humidity in a church is the moisture content of the outside air which finds its way in. This can be dominant if the church is well ventilated, and significant even if it is apparently sealed. With all windows shut and doors in normal use, infiltration rates are conventionally estimated at 0.25 air changes per hour for a large church (over 7000 m^3) and 0.5 in a smaller one, but actual figures can vary substantially. For instance, a small church could well have one air change per hour or more, while in King's College Chapel the measured rate was 1.5 per day.

In the UK heating season atmospheric relative humidities are commonly above 80% (figure 3.2); 100% is not unusual, particularly with westerly winds and at night. The absolute humidity of the air remains constant unless water vapour enters or leaves it by some mechanism, so if there is

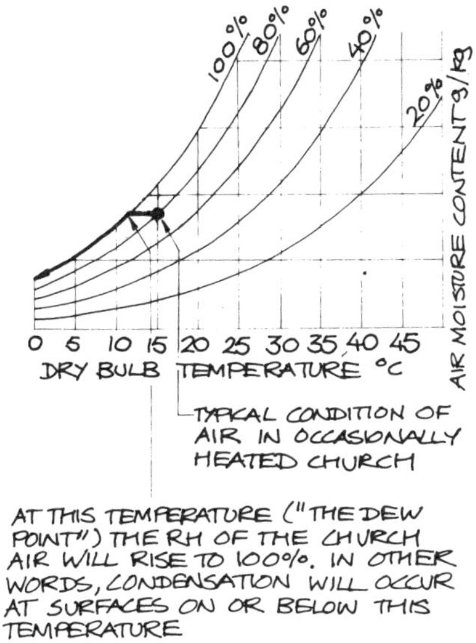

FIG. 3.3. THE CONDENSATION PROCESS

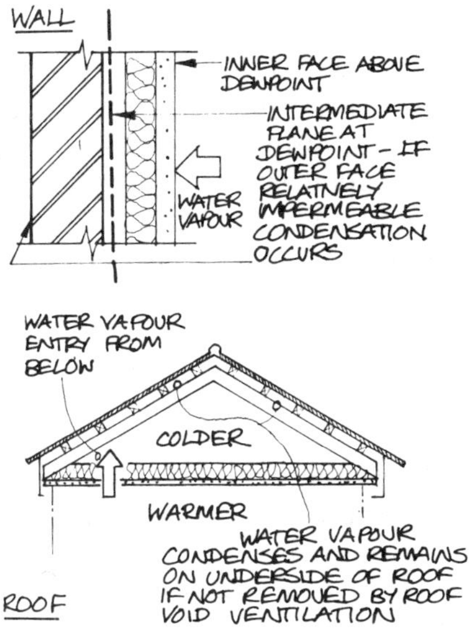

FIG. 3.4. INTERSTITIAL CONDENSATION

no change in moisture content, the resulting RH in the church may be determined from the psychrometric chart (viz figure 3.3).

For instance, if outside air at 4° C and 100% RH enters a building and is heated to the ambient temperature of say 14° C, its RH will fall to 50%. Conversely, in springtime the heating might be off and the building structure at the mean outside temperature, again say 14° C. If a warm front were to arrive at 20° C and 80% RH and this air filled the building, condensation would occur. Massive buildings near the west and south coasts are particularly prone to this 'warm weather condensation' and where this occurs one should consider dehumidification or heating when there is a rapid rise in external air temperature.

In an occasionally-heated church, provided there is no internal water vapour input, the expected relative humidity often averages about 75–80%. This is just below the danger limit but well above the optimum level. Unfortunately, there are numerous ways in which the moisture level may be raised, for instance:

Evaporation of water entering as rising damp, through structural defects, pipe leaks etc, or from flowers.

Transfer of moist air from immediately adjacent areas, such as a tank room, kitchen, severy or crowded church hall.

Metabolism, each person introducing about 50 grams of water vapour per hour; more when it is warm or when they are speaking or singing, or wearing wet clothes.

Combustion products from flueless heaters.

On the face of it, excessive relative humidities can easily be dealt with by heating though the cost may be high; the psychrometric chart shows that the higher the temperature for a given moisture content, the lower the RH. However, if moisture is being produced in the church faster than it can get out, it will build up. The normal method is to remove the excess by ventilation, particularly during and following the main periods of use, but this of course also removes heat. A small amount of water vapour will also escape by diffusion.

In practice certain materials, particularly wood, plaster and stone, stabilise the RH by absorbing water vapour from humid air and re-emitting it later. However, the rate of absorption may be slow in relation to the peak rate of output from congregations, tourists, and particularly flueless heaters, the total absorptive capacity is limited, and materials may suffer where RHs are consistently too high, too low, or fluctuate too much.

The occasionally-heated church is thus on the verge of being dangerously damp and good ventilation is necessary. Otherwise some small change, such as draughtproofing, leaks not attended to, or the introduction of flueless heaters, could be the last straw.

The alternative is dehumidification, often using a device which operates in a similar manner to a domestic refrigerator with the door left open, and uses many of the same components. The excess water vapour removed by condensation on a cooled coil runs off into the bucket or preferably to a drain, while the heat extracted is returned to the building through a second coil. The units cost relatively little to run in comparison with heating and ventilation to obtain the same rate of moisture removal, and give out a limited amount of heat themselves. Dehumidifiers have been used very little in churches to date, but wider application is now likely. They are most effective in winter and where ventilation rates are low, and more research is needed to determine exactly where they will be suitable and the correct size of equipment required. Impressive bucketsful of water do not necessarily represent a significant improvement in conditions.

In a more regularly heated church, the mean temperature will be higher and so high relative humidities are less likely. Indeed, in the past with continuous heating and stoves pulling large amounts of air through the church, excessively low RHs were often the problem, and this is still so in some warm and well-ventilated buildings today.

3.6. Arranging for Ventilation and Humidity Control

The specific balance between heating, ventilation and usage can cause such variations in relative humidity levels that it is best not to hypothesise. Quick checks can be made using a hygrometer and a maximum and minimum thermometer; these could usefully be installed as standard and inspected regularly. Portable recording instruments such as thermohygrographs are useful for surveys and modern electronic equipment is gaining ground. It is recommended that measurements are always made for several weeks in winter before and after any major changes to the heating system; potential hazards can often be overcome by small alterations to control settings and to ventilation arrangements, or possibly by use of a dehumidifier.

It will normally be best to have a little permanent background ventilation (unavoidable natural infiltration may be sufficient, particularly in smaller churches without damp problems, high occupancies or flueless heaters), with means of boosting where necessary, using either:

Wind pressure differences, particularly by cross-ventilation through grilles and windows, which may be fitted with mesh screens to keep birds out.

Natural buoyancy (the stack effect). Warm air rises and is expelled through high level openings, drawing in fresh air at low level. The ventilation rate increases the warmer the building, and can cause excessive heat loss where the air is well heated and stratifies. It is therefore most suitable with radiant and flueless systems.

Mechanical extraction. Measured rates can be established and automatically controlled according to conditions or to the use of the church. Fans require automatic dampers to prevent unnecessary infiltration and heat loss when they are off. Acoustic treatment will often be necessary if they are to run during occupancy periods. Fresh air heating and flued heating systems which draw combustion air from the church provide a degree of mechanical ventilation automatically.

Void spaces above ceilings and roofs, below suspended floors and in cavity walls are designed to be ventilated by outside air to disperse water vapour and avoid condensation. Air bricks, eaves and ridge ventilators to these spaces must never be blocked up. When ventilation rates to the church proper are reduced and heating and insulation is made more efficient, increased ventilation of voids may become necessary. Impervious tiles, foam carpet backings and underlays over timber floors may also inhibit such 'breathing'.

A general rule to help avoid moisture-related problems is to heat the church gently to keep internal surfaces above the dew point temperature of the outside air, and to provide sufficient ventilation to prevent any build-up of moisture. Many problems could be avoided if doors and windows were left open for a short time after each service: they now tend to be shut up tight for security and to keep in the valuable heat. There were less difficulties of this kind when churches were left open for occasional worshippers practically the whole time. Where necessary, it may be more convenient to use an extract fan on a timer; in suitable outdoor conditions, the fan may also be used to introduce warm, dry air into the church. However, where dehumidifiers are installed, ventilation rates will normally need to be kept to a minimum.

If condensation does not affect any building elements prone to rot or chemical attack, and if valuable objects are taken out or suitably protected, many methods of heating for comfort will prove satisfactory. However, care must be taken in making a choice: many advisers may be experts in heating, or in a certain type of heating, but not in building performance in general or conservation requirements in particular.

4. FUELS AND HEAT GENERATION

In this chapter we review fuels and their storage, combustion and effluent disposal problems. Coal burning is considered first, then oil, then gas, since most types of coal-burning appliance can be adapted to burn oil, and most types of oil burning appliance can also burn gas, but the reverse is not necessarily true. The results of converting existing coal and oil equipment to gas can be disappointing, however, since efficiencies may drop owing to different flame characteristics.

All fuel-burning and electrical equipment is potentially dangerous and safety must be the prime design requirement. Guidance is available from insurance companies and fire authorities, and there are building regulations and codes of practice to be complied with. Insurers should always be consulted before a heating system is installed or alterations are made. Larger heating equipment is usually separately insured and the policy requires regular inspections.

4.1. Fuel Choice

The following points are important when choosing between fuels.

Availability

Gas and electricity may not always be readily available, supply capacity may be limited, and there may be major local variations in the delivered cost of other fuels. The suppliers' initial statements should not be immediately accepted: improved terms can often be negotiated.

Maintenance and Attendance

Generally the cost of maintenance increases in the following order: electricity, natural gas, bottled gas, liquid fuel, solid fuel. Attendance costs are lowest for natural gas and electric systems, which are most easily controlled and maintained, and have no storage and delivery problems. Oil systems require regular cleaning and servicing to maintain efficiency. Solid fuel usually requires daily attendance, even where there is automatic stoking and de-ashing equipment.

Installation Requirements and Cost

As a general rule, equipment and installation costs increase in the order: electricity, gas, light oil, heavy oil, solid fuel. The choice is often, but by no means always, between high capital expenditure to keep running costs to a minimum or a lower initial outlay and higher operating costs.

Running Costs

The price of fuels is very susceptible to political and technical changes. For instance, gas used to be expensive, owing to costs additional to those of the coal and oil from which it was made. Then in the 1970s, the 'oil crisis' and North Sea development gave gas a major price advantage (figure 4.1). This advantage has now been diminished as a matter of government policy. Normally, it would be wiser to assume that the more convenient fuel, being more refined, will tend to be more expensive, and not to overemphasise current market conditions.

Future Flexibility

It is worth considering the adaptability of systems to different fuels. For instance, if there was little to choose in capital and running cost between unit heaters and a central system, the central system would normally be preferred, because a change in fuel could be made by altering the heat source only, retaining heat emitters and distribution systems.

Flexibility may also influence the location of equipment. For instance, a gas boiler can be located in many positions, and can use special types of flue. If these features are not essential, a wiser choice might be a conventional flue and a location where future supplies of solid or liquid fuel could be arranged.

Systems may also be designed for more than one type of fuel. For instance, a low pressure hot water system might use a small automatic solid fuel boiler or a heat pump as a gentle source of background heat and a gas or oil-fired unit as a booster. Multi-fuel boilers and stoves are also available, but they are not necessarily as efficient as single-purpose equipment and performance should be checked.

Equipment Characteristics

If a particular form of heating (for example high temperature radiant heating) appears technically the most suitable, it should not be rejected solely because the most appropriate fuel is not the cheapest.

4.2. Solid Fuels

Solid fuels are best suited for sustained demands in larger installations where sophisticated equipment and a suitable level of attendance is appropriate, or on a domestic scale where the user decides it is worth devoting his time to it.

Bituminous fuels contain volatile materials and require special equipment to burn cleanly. The more expensive smokeless fuels are generally used only in domestic appliances where elaborate burner design is not justified.

Transporting fuel and ash manually or mechanically is inconvenient and solid fuels must be stored close to the point of delivery and to the appliances served. This is often difficult, but a boiler house may be

FIG. 4.1. TYPICAL RELATIVE FUEL COSTS FOR SMALL CENTRAL HEATING SYSTEMS

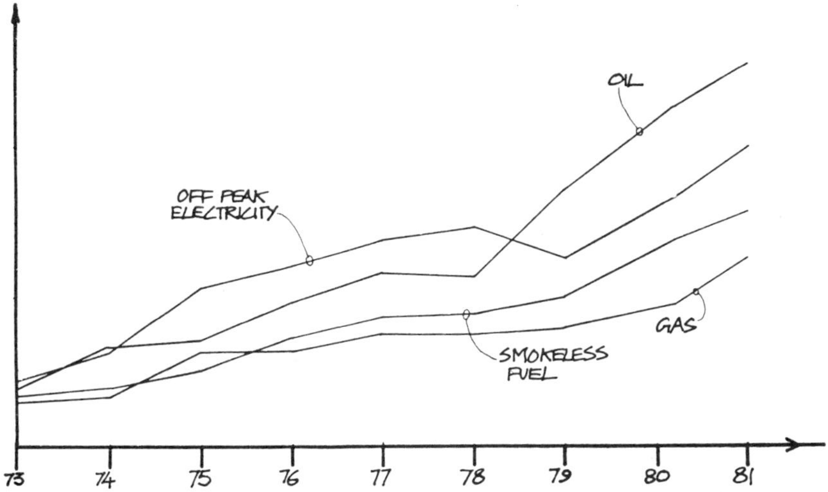

remote and hot water piped to the church. Solid fuel is bulky, particularly if the year's supply is purchased at low summer prices. The requirements should be carefully reviewed and suitable provision made: fuel heaped against a wall is unattractive and ultimately damages it.

The following automatic stokers are most commonly used in churches:

Gravity Feed
Smokeless fuel is burned on a sloping grate and automatically replenished from a hopper above. The hopper is reloaded and the ash removed about once a day. Thermostatic control is included and some advanced units can even extinguish and relight automatically.

Underfeed
A motorised feed screw brings fuel directly to the base of the burner. Volatile materials from bituminous fuel are driven off as the fuel is warmed, and oxidised as they pass through the incandescent bed, making the combustion smokeless.

Other types of stoker are available. Solid fuel may also be burned in pulverised form or in a fluidised bed, but available equipment is most suited to industrial use. Although modern appliances are more controllable and easier to operate, solid fuel is at its best for sustained heating needs. Where flexible automatic starting and stopping is required, other fuels will usually be preferred.

There is increasing interest in burning wood and waste products. This will seldom be practical in towns, owing to availability and smoke control. In the country, there may be opportunities to burn wood or straw. However:

relatively large volumes of fuel are required and so supplies, storage and handling requirements need to be assessed realistically

more maintenance and attendance is required than for other systems

soot accumulates rapidly, efficiency drops, and flues and chimneys become fire hazards if not cleaned and inspected frequently

burning waste manufactured goods produces toxic and corrosive fumes which may cause danger and damage.

4.3. Fuel Oil

Oil is supplied in many different grades. Generally, the more viscous and impure the grade, the cheaper it is, but the more the equipment and its operational and maintenance costs. Paraffin (Class C1) is used in flueless heaters, kerosene (Class C2) is used in domestic boilers, and gas oil/diesel oil (Class D) is used in medium sized boilers and air heaters. Heavier oils are not often used in churches today; they require more sophisticated burners and taller chimneys, need heating in order to flow, and their higher sulphur content increases the possibility of attack of stonework.

Prices can vary significantly with supplier and contract details, and competitive quotations should be obtained. It may be possible to join a purchasing group and enjoy bulk rates.

Oil tanks can be difficult to locate satisfactorily. Normal practice is to provide storage for three weeks' continuous operation. Potential suppliers should be consulted about filling arrangements, particularly if the proposed fill point is more than 18 metres from a suitable tanker position. Tanks need not be adjacent either to the boiler or to the fill point, but a compact layout is preferable.

The fill point is best located by the storage tank, to reduce the risk of undetected spillage. The fill pipe should fall continuously towards the tank or an isolating valve is necessary at the inlet. A reliable alarm, or preferably an interlock, is essential to protect against overflows. Exposed external oil lines should be insulated and possibly protected with heating tape, since Class D oil can freeze in abnormally cold weather.

Above-ground tanks are unsightly but may be camouflaged; provision should be made to inspect and paint all round. There is a small fire risk, so they should be away from lightning conductors and preferably windows. Corrosion-protected steel tanks may be buried, anchored where necessary to avoid displacement by groundwater, and with a manhole for periodic inspection. Reinforced concrete underground tanks with ceramic linings are long lasting but expensive.

There are three main types of oil burner:

Wicks burn quietly but are suitable only for the lightest oil (paraffin, Grade C1). They require regular attention and are only found in portable and domestic equipment.

Vapourising Burners are used in small boilers and stoves. The simplest and quietest (found in unit heaters, small domestic boilers and warm air units) uses natural draught and heat alone to vapourise the oil. The alternative forced draught or mechanical atomising devices are noisier.

Pressure Jet Burners permit precise control of combustion and are standard for larger installations which require good fuel economy and compliance with clean air regulations. Skilled maintenance is essential, at not more than six monthly intervals. The fuel, heated if necessary, is forced through an atomiser and mixes with blown air. Ignition is automatic, generally electric. The burners are noisy and equipment needs to be in its own room.

Where oil burners are at high level (e.g: in the tower) spillage could be catastrophic. A small daily service tank is therefore filled as required from the main reserve tank.

Oil feed lines are preferably of corrosion-protected steel, since this is not easily damaged. Vapourising burners may be gravity fed while pressure jets require pumps. Pumped transfer is generally preferred as a leak is less likely to cause a major flood.

Heating oils do not ignite unless heated or vapourised by other means.

Internal tanks are placed in fire-resisting chambers, ventilated to the outside air, with a catchpit to retain the entire contents plus a safety margin. Catchpits are occasionally required for external tanks, especially where leakage could enter the church or adjoining properties.

If there is a fire, or if the burner fails to light, oil must be shut off. Integral burner controls allow for most eventualities but a fire valve should also be installed; this is held open by a wire containing fusible links which melt at about 60° C, with a manual quick-release device. Fire valves are also a useful precaution with high-rated gas-fired equipment.

4.4. Natural Gas

Gas is currently relatively low in cost, no storage is required, it can often be burnt quietly in the church itself in a variety of unit heaters, and equipment and flues are relatively simple to install and monitor. Natural gas is not poisonous, but there is an explosion risk. Safety interlocks are incorporated in British Gas Approved appliances to avoid leakage of unburnt gas and the Area Board's published safety precautions should be followed if any leakage is suspected. Installation is subject to the Gas Act and Gas Safety Regulations.

Supplies from nearby mains should not be taken for granted: there may be high connection charges or limitations on available capacity. Tariffs can vary and should be discussed with the Area Board at an early stage.

Gas meters should be at ground level in a well-ventilated area, as near as possible to the site boundary. For larger installations, the supply authority may require a separate meter house near the boundary line. Since gas is metered by volume, the cooler the meter position the more fuel is obtained for a given price.

Gas is suited not only for conventional stoves and boilers but for direct radiant and air heating equipment. Two main types of burner are used:

Atmospheric burners are widely used on small convector stoves and radiant heaters and on some larger heaters and boilers; they are usually quiet, although ignition noise can be distracting. Some units have fan-assisted draught which gives more flexibility in flueing and can improve efficiency by avoiding heat loss to excess combustion air, particularly where a boiler is on low fire or off. Ignition is preferably electrical in order to avoid fuel wastage.

Forced Draught gas burners are similar to oil pressure jets, and are normally the more efficient. They are essential in systems where

FIG. 4.2. BALANCED FLUES

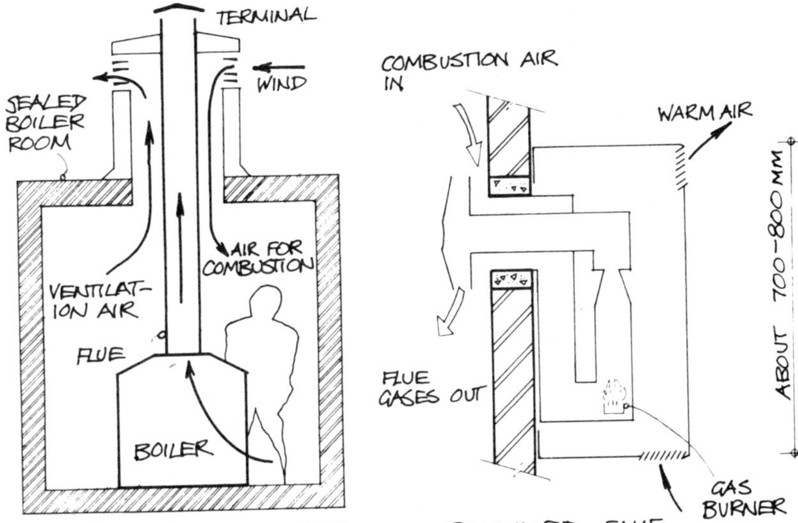

BALANCED FLUE– SEALED BOILER ROOM

BALANCED FLUE HEATER

FIG. 4.3. DILUTION FLUES

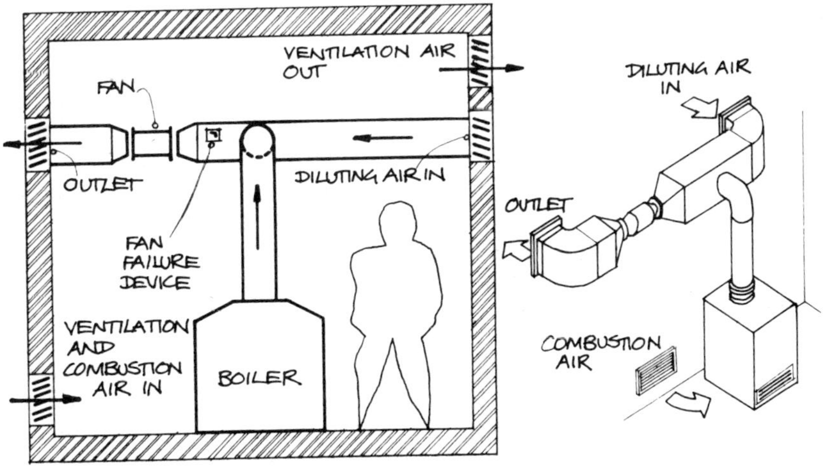

other fuels may be burned, either in a multi-fuel boiler or in order to simplify future conversion.

Alternative types of flue are available for gas and some small oil heaters, which can make their installation more convenient. Some heaters have no flue at all, discharging relatively innocuous combustion products into the heated space. These are discussed further in Section 5.4.

Balanced Flues (figure 4.2) are widely used in domestic gas boilers and room heaters. The burner obtains combustion air and discharges fumes through a wall or roof terminal, designed to equalise any wind pressure differences. In favourable circumstances, conventional gas and light oil boilers may also be installed in a sealed compartment with the air intake surrounding the flue terminal. Fan assisted balanced flue heaters are also available; the smaller flue size increases flexibility in installation, and with good designs the better control of combustion air volume raises overall boiler efficiency.

Dilution Flues (figure 4.3) provide a fan-assisted stream of air in a duct into which the fumes are discharged and diluted to a safe concentration to be blown out through a grille.

At low outside temperatures and high relative humidities, water vapour discharged may form a fog around balanced and dilution flue wall terminals. Although normally harmless, visually it can be a nuisance.

4.5. Liquefied Petroleum Gas

Liquefied bottled gas is an expensive alternative to natural gas, but is useful where there are no mains supplies and for self-contained portable equipment. Leakage is a fire and explosion risk: cylinders should be stored in limited quantities away from combustible materials in a well-ventilated place, preferably outside, and all equipment, pipe and hose connections should be well maintained and regularly inspected. The widespread use of flueless gas appliances may also cause problems as discussed in Chapter 5.

For larger installations, liquefied petroleum gas may be delivered by tanker and stored in large spheres or cylinders. Since the gas tends to lie on the ground when released, bulk storage vessels must be away from buildings, fenced in or otherwise isolated from tampering, and open to the air; they can be obtrusive and are best concealed by planting. Prices may vary considerably depending on demand and the use made of the fuel locally.

4.6. Electricity

Electric heating often has the lowest installed cost but the high price of standard rate electricity often limits applications to local and occasional heating requirements. It is very useful for bringing heat, particularly radiant heat, to occupants rather than heating the whole building.

If the electricity is used efficiently, off-peak rates can be comparable with other heating fuels. Since the off-peak period is usually in the small hours, the heat normally has to be stored. However, the high thermal capacity and slow response of many churches may permit off-peak electricity to be used directly to take the chill off in the early hours.

Tariffs and supply arrangements should be negotiated with the Area Board at an early stage before any choice of equipment and operating procedures is agreed. Some Area Electricity Boards offer a weekend restricted hours tariff or an evening and weekend 'Community Tariff' at reduced rates. Where heating systems are efficient and the necessary supply capacity is available, this can permit cost-effective intermittent electric heating. Outside the weekend or evening periods, charges are at or above the standard rate.

For the larger electrical consumer, a maximum demand tariff charges for the highest rate of consumption as well as the total amount of electricity used. This tariff is seldom appropriate for churches, as it proves expensive where electric heating is intermittently or occasionally used. Tariffs should be reviewed from time to time; it is not unusual to find that a consumer is paying too much. Area Boards do not take the initiative in suggesting changes, but respond helpfully on request.

Electricity may be converted into heat by the following means.

Direct Resistance Heating

The current is passed through resistance wires suspended in a protective enclosure. Examples are electric convectors, air heater batteries and many radiant heaters.

Indirect Resistance Heating

The resistance element heats a material which in turn gives out heat. Examples are floor heating, immersion heaters, oil-filled electric radiators, tubular and lamp heaters. The potentially hazardous electric element is separated from the outside environment and can be fitted with an added safety device, such as a high temperature cut-out; they are therefore generally to be preferred in churches.

Storage Heating

Resistance elements also heat blocks in off-peak storage heaters; the fan assisted versions can be useful where a quick boost is required, though economic control is difficult, particularly for buildings in occasional use. Off-peak electricity may also be used in purpose-designed systems using building elements (particularly floors) or tanks of water for heat storage.

Heat Pumps

Electricity (or indeed other fuels) may be used in a refrigeration system in reverse to take heat out of the outside air, or from a ground or water source (for example, a lake) and transfer it into a building by means of warm air or warm water; this allows more heat to be transferred than its equivalent in fuel consumed. However, the fuel is normally the expensive on-peak electricity and the heat is at a low temperature (generally 60° C or less) which restricts applications to warm air and low temperature convection and radiant heating. The ratio between the heat output and the energy consumed is known as the Coefficient of Performance. Heat pumps are worth considering in special circumstances and for new, intensively used, well insulated buildings, but they are not yet very suitable for occasional heating requirements. Controls, reliability and quoted Coefficients of Performance need to be carefully scrutinised for all intended applications.

4.7. Solar Heating

Solar heating is topical, but currently special collectors and heat transfer systems are only cost-effective for sustained year-round needs, for example in swimming pools and occasionally for domestic hot water systems. Passive solar heating – using the building to trap the sun's heat – is traditional and may be used to advantage, particularly in new buildings. The simplest method is to use south-facing windows, with suitable methods of shading them to avoid glare and overheating problems, and inbuilt thermal capacity to store the heat. In existing buildings, it may be possible to make use of the warm air which frequently accumulates in the roof space on sunny days by using a thermostatically-controlled fan to blow it into the church. This will also help to maintain even temperatures and to reduce relative humidities within the church but will not eliminate the need for a conventional heating system.

5. HEAT EMITTERS

Here we describe heating systems starting with the heat emitter rather than, as is more conventional, the fuel and type of system. The heat emitters are initially classified according to whether their primary mode of heat output is to radiation or to the air. Other relevant classifications are then considered, particularly flueless and local heating. Central heating and controls are dealt with in later chapters.

Unfortunately, certain heaters, otherwise technically satisfactory, look ugly. This is more a problem of product design than of technical requirements. Users should encourage manufacturers to make improvements; some will depart from their standard ranges if pressed, or may be interested in developing new products. More collective action by groups of potential customers will help to accelerate this development.

5.1. Radiant Heaters

All radiant heaters produce electromagnetic radiation, largely in the infra-red, which is identical to light in all but wavelength. The radiation is emitted spontaneously from any heated object, the total quantity increasing rapidly and the average wavelength reducing as it becomes hotter.

Radiant heaters may be placed in four groups according to wavelength: short wave (white heat), medium wave (red heat), long wave (black heat) and low temperature thermal (normal hot water temperatures). The first three types usually have very hot elements and produce intense radiation which may ignite materials placed too close to them; they must therefore be installed and positioned with great care. The shorter the wavelength the more compact the source (size ratios for the four classifications being approximately 1:20:300:4000) and the greater the proportion of radiation to total heat output. Short wave sources, being small, can potentially be focused very well; medium wave sources quite well, long wave moderately, and thermal hardly at all. Reflectors, where fitted, should be kept clean.

Air is relatively transparent to short wave radiation but components, particularly water vapour, absorb some longer wavelengths more strongly. The absorption increases with absolute humidity and adds to the inevitable fall-off in radiant intensity with distance making it important to keep radiant heaters fairly close to the people, even though aesthetically this may be difficult.

The absorption is much less important for short wave heaters. There is also some evidence that people feel more comfortable with the short-wave radiation, and that greater intensities and greater asymmetry is possible with short wave heaters. Psychologically, this may be because the radiation's characteristics are closer to those of sunlight. Physically and physiologically, the short wave radiation penetrates clothing and the skin more deeply, thus being absorbed more uniformly and to some extent passing directly into the bloodstream.

Radiant heaters have an immediate effect on thermal comfort without first having to warm the building or the air. Fast responding units are thus well-suited to occasional-heating needs and to improving conditions in small parts of an otherwise unheated, or poorly-heated building. Nevertheless, the building may not feel comfortable if the air and surfaces are too cold (see Chapter 2). Valuable objects should not be exposed to too much radiation as they may be damaged, particularly through the associated drying effect.

Short Wave Radiant Heaters (figure 5.1.)

Short wave heaters are necessarily electric, relying either on electronic processes or on high temperatures not attainable by normal burners. The most common types are lamps, designed to reduce the proportion of visible light in the beam and to let out more of the infra-red radiation. They give out about half as much visible light as a tungsten lamp of a similar rating, but any temptation to use the heaters as the sole source of light should be resisted. Where the light is an embarrassment, filters may be fitted: these reduce the efficiency slightly. A red glow remains which draws attention to the source but little more.

The lamps most commonly used are:

Mushroom-shaped with integral reflectors. These are similar in design to spotlight bulbs, with relatively low outputs. They can be useful for local needs, for example to make things a bit more comfortable in the pulpit or for the organist.

Tubular with external reflectors. These have higher outputs (1000 – 3000 watts each), and units with multiple lamps can heat several hundred square feet (tens of square metres) at a time.

The lamps deliver their full output very soon after switching-on and are in many ways ideal for intermittent comfort heating requirements, provided their appearance is acceptable and electrical supplies have the necessary capacity. As with most radiant heaters, they should be

FIG. 5.1. SHORT WAVE RADIANT HEATERS

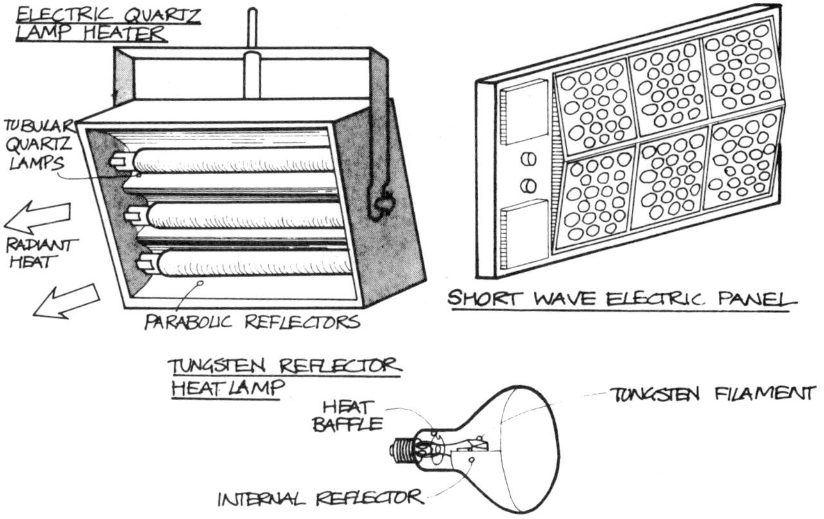

FIG. 5.2. MEDIUM WAVE RADIANT HEATERS

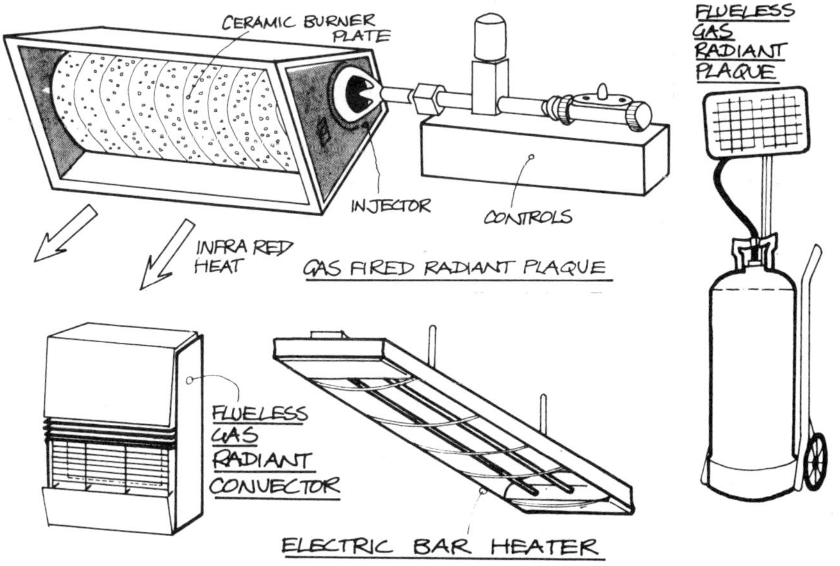

switched on a little before occupation in order to help warm up the floor and seats. Although good at improving comfort locally, they do not heat the building or the air much generally, so there may be problems of dampness unless there is either background heating (with suitable ventilation) or dehumidification. Owing to the relatively high cost of electricity, they are less economic for more sustained heating needs.

Flat panel short wave heaters produce the physiologically more acceptable short wave radiation with no visible component and without themselves getting very hot. Unlike the lamp heaters, the radiation is diffuse, making them more suitable for small rooms and sometimes as an alternative to low temperature electric panels.

Medium Wave Radiant Heaters (figure 5.2.)

Medium wave heaters are characterised by their red to yellow glow and have their antecedents in open coal and wood fires. Today, the main fuels are gas and electricity.

The electric heaters frequently have coiled elements enclosed in silica tubes, with a reflector behind; they are usually attached to walls or suspended from the ceiling. Being relatively low in output, they are most often used for local heating.

The gas-fired units are more powerful, with ceramic radiant elements heated directly by the flame, as in a domestic gas fire. They are usually mounted at high level for safety and to get a good spread of radiation. Since there are no reflectors the radiation is less focused than with the electric heaters. Gas-fired radiants are widely used for fast-responding heating of large areas, the heating effects being partly by direct radiation, partly re-radiation from other surfaces, and partly from direct and indirect heating of the air. There is ignition noise and a slight hissing from the burners. Most available units are flueless, the combustion products helping to warm the air. However, in some circumstances flueless heaters can give problems, as discussed in Section 5.4.

Portable flueless units are available for bottled gas, ranging from the small floor-standing domestic heater to industrial units with a large cylinder at the base and the element at the end of a long neck. They are a useful temporary expedient but are not recommended for the long term: fixed apparatus is safer.

Long Wave Radiant Heaters (figure 5.3.)

Long wave heaters are mounted at high level on walls or suspended from ceilings; horizontal mounting is best as it minimises heat loss by

FIG. 5.3. LONG WAVE RADIANT HEATERS

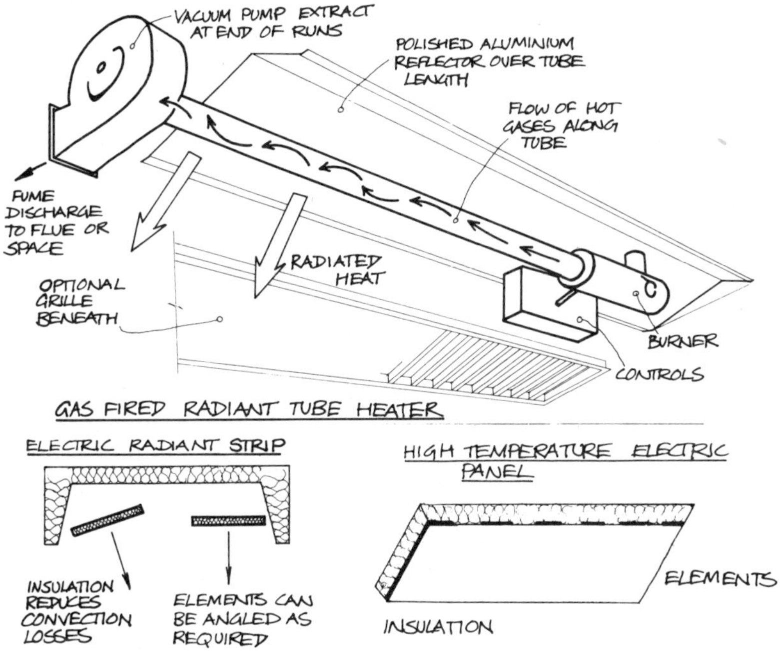

FIG. 5.4. LOW TEMPERATURE RADIANT HEATERS

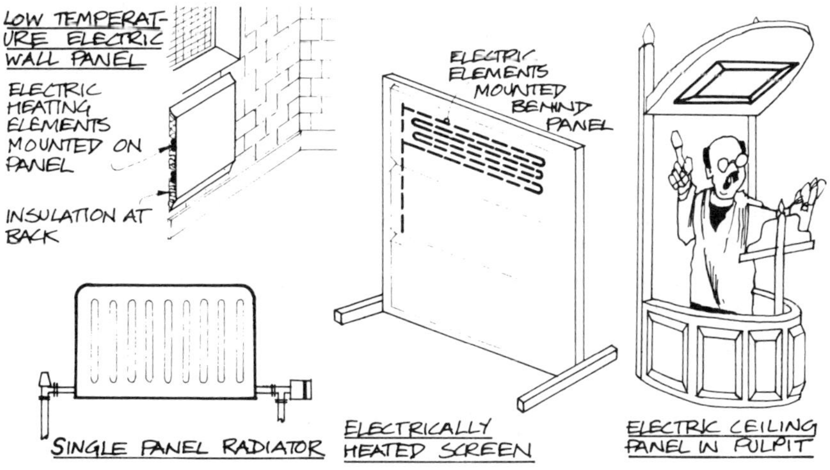

convection. At about 300° C, their surfaces do not give off visible radiation but can nevertheless ignite organic materials. The necessary radiant surface area for a given output is larger and the heaters often take a linear form, which can sometimes be easier to accommodate architecturally than individual units. Again, the most widely-used fuels are gas and electricity.

In the gas-fired units, a fan draws the combustion gases from the burner through a tube mounted in front of a reflector. Heat is transferred from the gases to the tube and then re-radiated and re-convected into the church. The units may be either modular, with a straight or U-tube, or linear, with a fan at the end of a long tube and a number of burners along its length.

The heaters may be either flued or flueless: flueing is recommended and is easier for the linear system where fume extract is centralised, than for multiple small units. A flued system drawing combustion air from within the church is usually best as it avoids problems with combustion gases and provides limited mechanical ventilation. Noise can originate from air intakes, burners, extract fans, and from thermal expansion and contraction of the tubes and reflectors, but can usually be minimised by careful selection and design. The fan can, if necessary, be silenced and mounted outside.

Electric black heaters are available in strip or panel form. Their main advantage is their unobtrusiveness: the poorer radiation characteristics and the absence of reflectors makes them generally less efficient and less suitable for occasional heating than short and medium wave units, while for more sustained heating, gas heaters would often be more economic. One type of strip heater has adjustable elements allowing limited control over the direction of the radiation.

High pressure hot water or steam pipes, with or without reflectors, are also useful long wave radiant sources. The temperatures are lower and the surface areas required several times larger than for the gas and electric systems, but they are not a fire risk. High pressure systems were widely used in churches during the last century, but are now uncommon owing to more rigorous safety requirements.

Low Temperature Radiant Heaters (figure 5.4.)
Low temperature radiant heaters fall into two main groups: panels which operate at normal hot water temperatures (45 – 80° C) and wall, floor and ceiling heating with surfaces only a few degrees above room

temperature. Many only just qualify to be called radiant, as much of their output goes directly into the air and structure of the building.They are most suitable either for localised heating or where the building and the air are to be warmed generally, but the additional radiation makes it possible to be comfortable at a rather lower air temperature.

The most common examples are the hot water single panel radiator and various electric heating panels. About 50% of their heat output is by radiation, although unless the radiator is free-standing nearly half falls on the wall behind. For hot water radiators this may be reduced by insulation or aluminium foil placed at the back; this also cuts overall heat output and panel sizes may need increasing accordingly. However, uninsulated electric panels should never be adapted on site as they will overheat.

To get full advantage of the radiation, panels should be placed above head level, but this is not always practical. However, if mounted nearer the floor, they can overheat the people nearby while hardly being noticed by those further away. They are therefore best used either for whole church heating, positioned a little away from seats, or close by at low output for very local heating.

5.2. Ceiling, Floor and Wall Heating (figure 5.5.)

Wall, ceiling and floor warming are invisible forms of low temperature radiant heating, the Roman hypocaust being the historical precedent. Today, hot water or electric heating elements may be embedded in walls, ceilings or floors, or placed behind them. This form of heating causes no staining, and by improving radiant temperatures, permits comfortable conditions to be achieved at lower air temperatures. However, it is usually expensive, and often slow-responding, having to warm the structure first, and thus most suitable for continuously-heated buildings. If buried heating elements are damaged or break down, repair or replacement is often disruptive and expensive.

Embedded hot water wall panels were popular in the 1930s, but were expensive to install, difficult to maintain, and increased heat losses; they will not be considered further.

Ceiling heating is normally provided either by electric heating mats behind plasterboard, or by hot water pipe coils behind a metal ceiling. Very good insulation is required above to avoid excessive heat loss. The air immediately below a heated ceiling is not particularly hot since heat can only move down by conduction, radiation and forced circulation; the main mechanism of heat emission (provided the ceiling is horizontal) is by radiation to the floor. Possible applications in existing churches are very limited.

Floor heating can sometimes be considered in new buildings and with major alterations it can help produce good comfort in continuously heated buildings without stratification, but is generally inappropriate for intermittent heating. The slow rate of response also makes it better for background heating than for full heating, when temperature overshoots occur, leading to discomfort and energy waste. Floor temperatures are limited to about 25°C (77°F) in spaces where people are for several hours, but may be increased to about 28°C (82°F) for intermittent occupancies and in circulation areas; otherwise there may be complaints of swollen feet. Consequently the maximum heat output is about 70 watts per square metre, and supplementary heat is usually necessary in tall spaces, existing poorly-insulated buildings and under large windows to counteract downdraughts and the 'cold' radiant effect.

Off-peak electric floor warming, popular in the 1960s, fell from favour largely through inflexibility of control and increases in fuel costs. Improved technology and better-insulated buildings are creating some new interest, though a hot water system will often be preferred in order to widen future fuel choice. Electric heater cables may be embedded or withdrawable; withdrawable is best to simplify repairs.

Floor warming by hot water is enjoying renewed popularity in well-insulated buildings, owing to advances in pipe materials, underfloor insulation, and new types of concrete screeds. The new systems respond faster and can also make good use of low temperature hot water from heat pumps. Small bore pipes are buried in continuous lengths, joints being made in header ducts or preferably in a manifold. Steel tube was used traditionally, owing to its low cost and good resistance to damage during installation. Copper then became more popular, being in long coils and with better corrosion resistance; plastic coatings are now available for further protection. Plastic tube alone is widely used in Continental Europe; experience in this country is growing but not all water authorities approve it. Installation is simplified using proprietary insulation panels complete with pipe supports. Installation and screeding should always be by specialist contractors who give a long term warranty.

Alternatively, lightweight timber or metal panels, incorporating insulation and pipe coils or other heating elements, may be placed over an existing floor. Similar electric systems are feasible, or warm air may

FIG. 5.5. CEILING & FLOOR HEATING

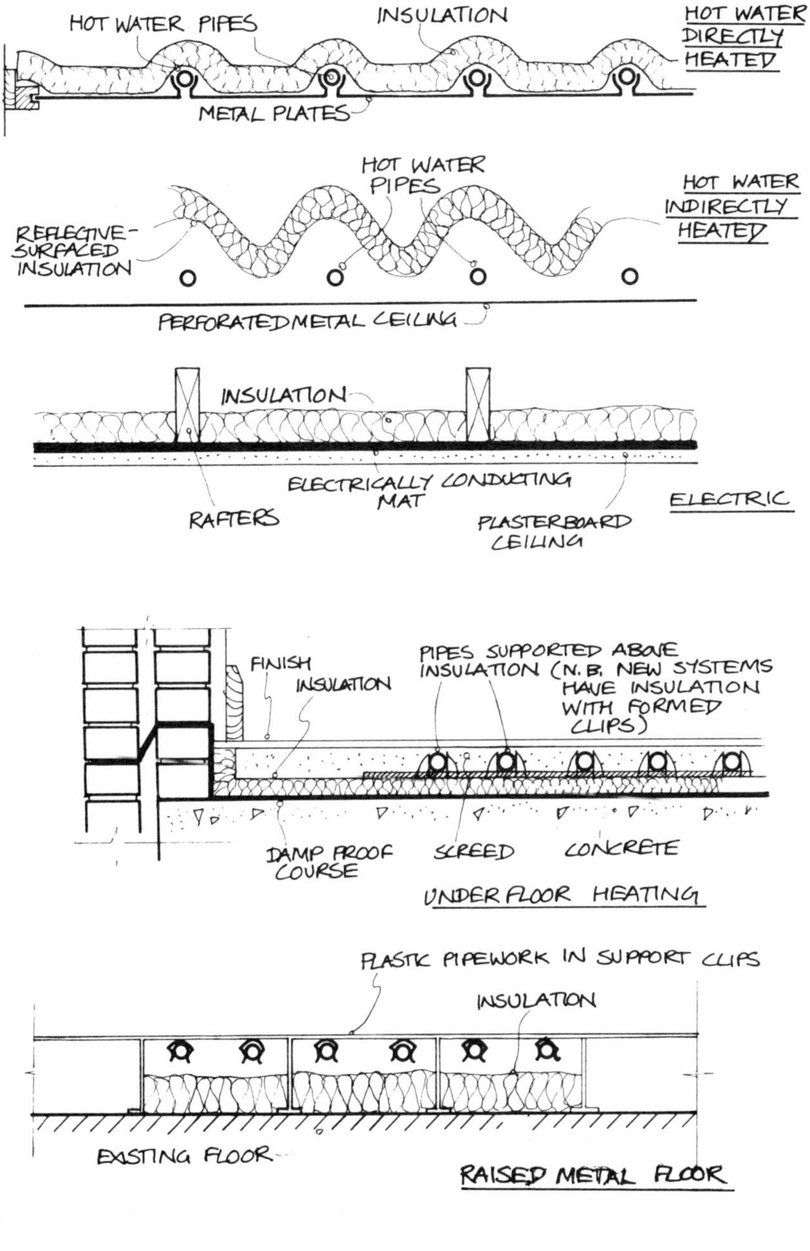

be circulated through a void. These faster-responding systems may also be used to improve thermal comfort locally.

Hot water underfloor systems require careful control of circulating temperatures, owing to problems of thermal expansion, overheating, and possible damage to plastics. The floor covering affects the output and the heating affects the floor finish: details may need amending. For instance, stone and marble slabs must be continuously bedded (not placed on dabs), drying-out requirements and adhesives must be suitably specified, and any subsequent changes to floor coverings can cause problems. Specification advice should be sought from installation specialists and the heating and flooring manufacturers.

5.3. Convective Heaters

Most heaters are predominantly convective, including many so-called radiators. There are two main types: natural convectors which use the buoyancy of warm air to promote heat transfer and forced convectors which use a fan.

Natural Convection

The main problem with natural convectors is also the mechanism by which they work: hot air rises. In tall spaces, this frequently makes the temperature high up in the vault much greater than that in the nave (figure 5.6). This stratification not only deprives the occupied part of the church of heat but also increases the overall heat loss, owing both to the greater temperature differences and to the additional air infiltration induced (see figure 9.2). To add insult to injury, the convection currents established often cause draughts.

Common types of natural convector are outlined in the following paragraphs. The more extended vertically and the hotter the convecting surface the more buoyant the air emerging and the greater the resulting air velocities and likely draughts. High temperature and high output units, although attractively compact, can be disappointing in their results; more gentle, less concentrated sources are preferable for tall spaces.

Solid Fuel Stoves Within the Church

Solid fuel stoves were widely used in churches, but today their applications are limited by the labour required. The heat output from an open fire is largely radiant, most of the convected heat going up the chimney. The casing of a stove restricts the flow of excess air, is warmed by convection, and intercepts most of the radiation, re-emitting the heat

FIG. 5.6. HEATING AND STRATIFICATION

through convection and lower temperature radiation. Convection tends to dominate with modern equipment where the casing is cool for safety. Heat output is usually concentrated and convection currents are severe.

Oil, Gas and Electric Stoves

Most modern units are light and compact, with relatively high air discharge temperatures. Where they are operated locally or intermittently in large and tall spaces, they may cause bad draughts and stratification. More massive units tend to produce a gentler heat, with a greater radiant component, but their high thermal capacity and slow response makes them less suited to intermittent heating. Where the oil and gas heaters are flueless, possible effects of the fumes and water vapour need to be taken into account.

Radiators

Radiators range from traditional cast-iron types to the ubiquitous pressed steel. Non-traditional materials are also available, including copper, aluminium and plastic; advantages are claimed but there are also problems. For instance, mixed metals in a system may promote corrosion, and new materials may deteriorate over time and can be more easily damaged. Robust products should be specified: some domestic radiators have only a 10-year design life. Radiators take four main forms (figure 5.7):

Column, with a battery of vertical fins.

Single Panel, with a flat or corrugated plate.

Multiple Panel, with several single panels connected to a common header.

Radiant Convector, normally a flat panel with profiled convective elements added.

Single panel radiators give the best ratio of radiant to convected heat (approximately 1:1) and the lowest tendency to stratification. Radiant convectors can be very useful at skirting level and for downdraught prevention, and modern patterns can be unobtrusive. Metallic paint should not normally be applied to radiators as it cuts the radiant heat output.

Convectors

Air enters at the base of the unit and emerges at the top or front; front discharge reduces the risk of staining walls. Low surface temperatures limit the radiant output but are safer and avoid roasting people close by. Convectors give great flexibility to obtain a given heat output and air discharge temperature in a restricted space, but the resulting heat and air distribution is not always good, particularly in tall churches and in the centre of wide churches with perimeter systems. Skirting convectors are useful and unobtrusive, but need careful specification to withstand wear and tear.

Plain or Finned Tube

Old installations frequently use plain cast iron pipe. The large volume of water contained makes the systems slow to respond and the heating surface is often too small for today's requirements. Where pipes run under floor grilles, the output is further decreased, especially when ducts are filled with dust and dirt. Pipe coils beneath windows can be effective at reducing downdraughts, but compact convectors are usually preferable. Finned or gilled tube emits more heat than plain but is normally best concealed, though sometimes its industrial appearance can work architecturally. Its heat output drops when dirty and cleaning should be arranged every few years.

FIG. 5.7. RADIATORS & NATURAL CONVECTORS

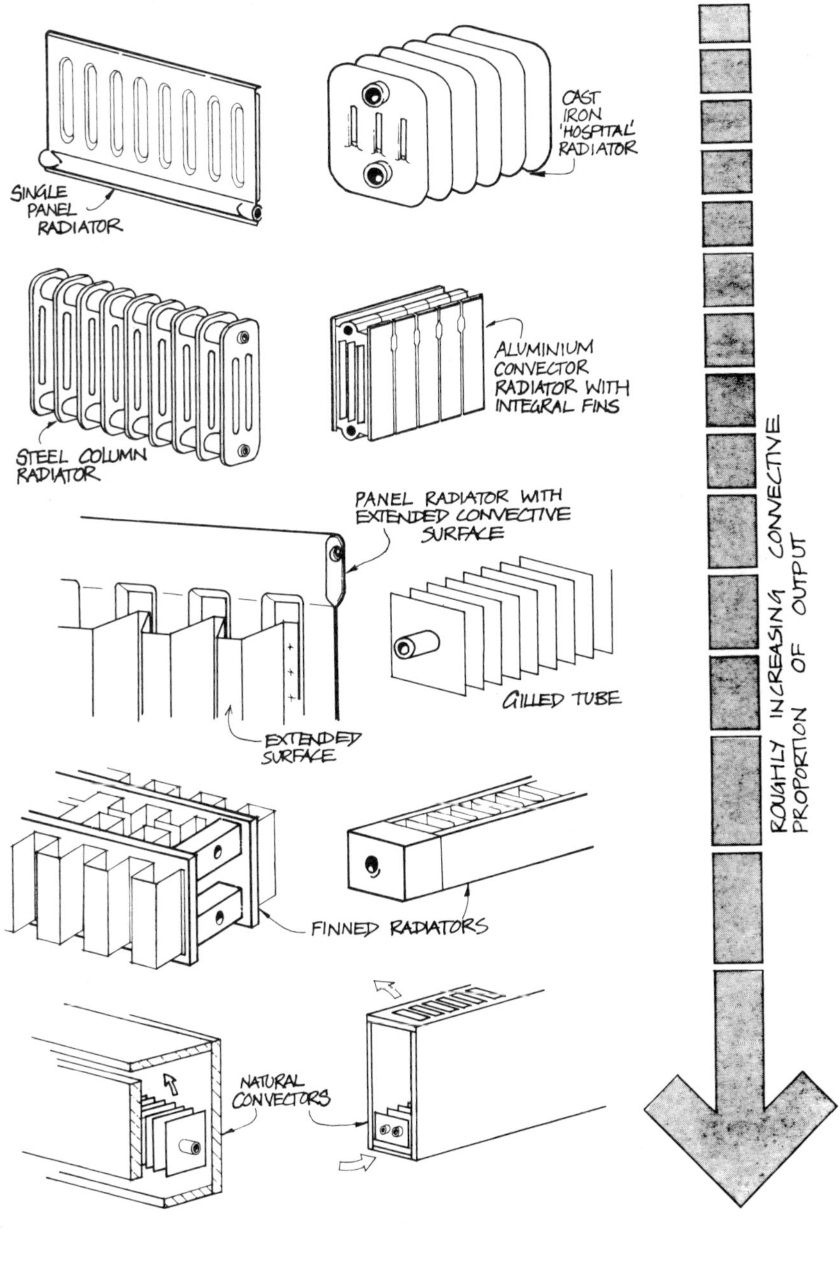

Forced Convectors and Warm Air Units (figure 5.8.)

Fans pass air over a heat exchanger, which may be heated directly by electricity or a burner, or indirectly by hot water or steam. There are also flueless oil and gas-fired units (often confusingly called direct air heaters), where the air is passed over the flame itself. Gas and oil-fired burners, particularly the larger ones, may be noisy and their performance should be checked carefully and comparable working installations visited before making a selection.

For a given output, forced convectors are smaller than natural convectors; they also give more control over the temperature, velocity and distribution of the warm air, which can help to reduce draughts and stratification in a well-designed system. Some design guidelines are discussed in Section 6.5. Where necessary, heaters may be located remotely and the air ducted to supply and return air grilles. Filters should be fitted, (and regularly maintained) to protect heat exchangers from clogging with dust, to reduce staining and increase the life of decorations generally.

Discomfort, and damage to organs etc., can sometimes arise from hot, dry discharged air or by rapid changes in relative humidity. Discharge temperatures must not be too low or there will be draughts, and fans should be arranged not to operate if no heat is available; a low temperature cut-out attached to the heat exchanger is often fitted as standard. Cool air may also be circulated in summer by switching on the fans only, though the improvement in comfort is usually minimal.

Although forced warm air systems may be sized to heat the air in the church very rapidly, care has to be taken in design. A quick blast of hot air may create an uncomfortable stuffy environment with a high air temperature, low radiant temperatures, and cold feet. The resulting rapid changes in relative humidity may also have adverse effects on the building and its contents.

Fan Convectors

The smaller fan-assisted units, with ratings between about 2 and 15 kilowatts, are known as fan convectors. They are most commonly heated by hot water. Gas-fired balanced flue units are also available and particularly suitable for smaller churches: one popular type has an efficiency of over 80% and a flue only 80 mm in diameter. Electric fan heaters are useful for rapid air heating in small rooms, but for larger spaces radiants will normally be more effective.

FIG. 5.8. FORCED AIR CONVECTORS AND WARM AIR UNITS

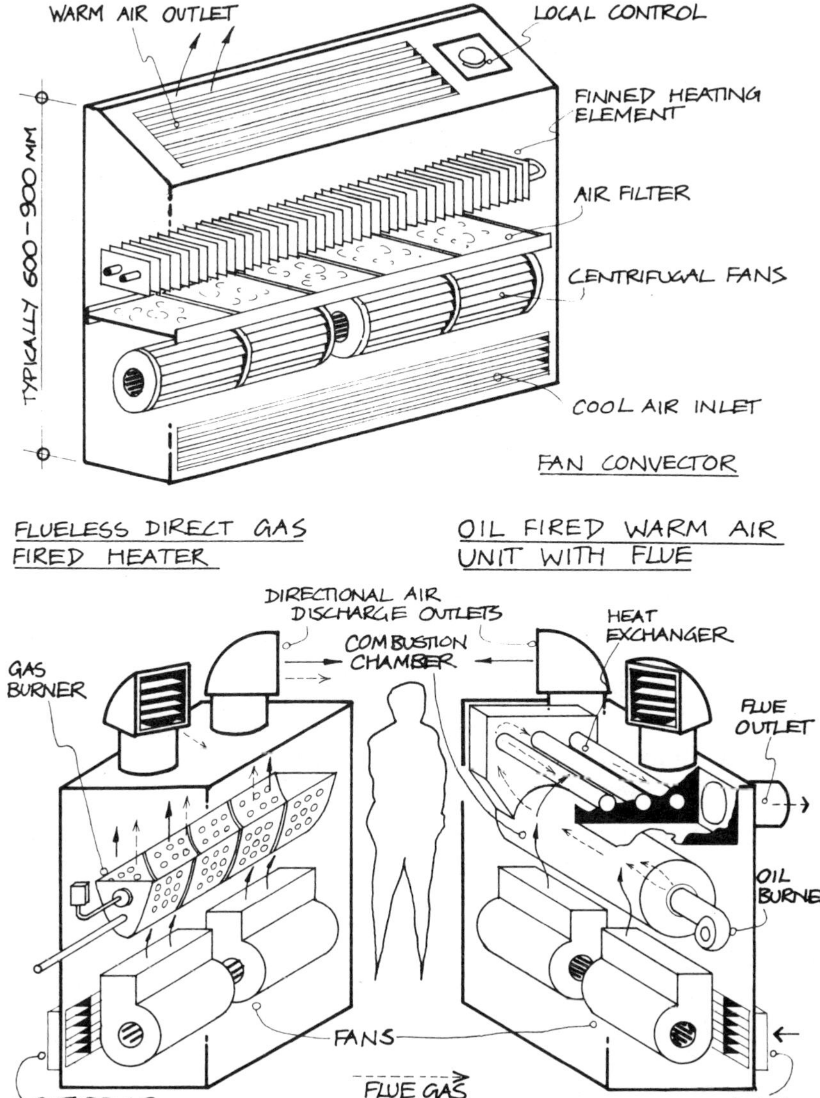

Outputs are normally catalogued with fans running at high speed, but noise levels may only be acceptable at low speed, and selection must take both into account. It may be possible to use the high fan speed for quicker warm-up before the church is occupied, with centralised manual or automatic change-over to low speed. However, with hot water systems, there may not always be the boiler capacity to meet the heat demands of high speed running. Many units have integral thermostats, usually detecting return air temperature. However, these are often rather crude and can lead to wide temperature fluctuations (see Chapter 7).

Air may be discharged from the top, bottom or front of fan convectors or through ductwork and diffusers. Except where used to overcome downdraughts, front or bottom discharge is best to avoid stratification and to project warm air towards the congregation initially. In one installation (figure 5.9) the air is discharged through long slots at the base of the units and is projected across the floor in a thin film; this not only keeps the warm air down but also heats up the surface of the floor before occupation. However, it requires a relatively unobstructed floor to work effectively (e.g. not too many hassocks).

Warm Air Units

Higher capacity warm air units, gas or oil fired, are widely used industrially and offer a simple, low cost means of heating the air rapidly. In relation to a carefully-designed system, they tend to be noisy, with poor air distribution and high hourly running cost. However, when used as a low cost replacement for elderly and inefficient central heating, they have often improved comfort with reduced running costs owing to the fewer hours of operation.

Warm air units may also be used in a more refined manner as the heat source in ducted systems, which are discussed in the next Chapter.

5.4. Flueless Heaters

Certain gas, paraffin and light oil unit heaters are designed to discharge combustion products directly into the church. The units are relatively low in capital cost and low running costs are claimed, since no heat is lost through a flue. However, selection must be made with some caution as problems can often arise from water vapour and occasionally from trace chemicals in the combustion products.

The following heat outputs produce approximately one litre of water vapour per hour:

Paraffin and bottled gas	8 kilowatts
Natural gas	7 kilowatts
Coal gas	2 kilowatts

The high rate of vapour production by coal gas is one reason why high ventilation rates were common in Victorian times, with gas lighting.

The water vapour is particularly troublesome with intermittent heating where flueless heaters are used exclusively. When the church is cold, the internal surfaces will often be close to dew point temperature. When the heaters come on, they immediately start producing water vapour. If air rising from the units meets cold wall surfaces, or collects in recesses where there is little air movement, condensation is likely. In any event, good ventilation is essential.

Flueless heating is ideally used as a local top-up to background heat by other indirect means. Where it is used alone, ventilation must be good, preferably mechanical, with extract at high level where the warmer and more humid air tends to accumulate. The temptation to use a large number of heaters to provide a rapid warm-up must be resisted, particularly with radiant units, as the absolute humidity of the air will rise rapidly before either the air of the surfaces of many building elements are warmed, and dew point conditions are easily reached. Condensation risk is reduced if units are switched on progressively, giving a gradually increasing output.

The level of other gaseous pollutants depends on the fuel burned, the burner characteristics, and the ratio of heat output to ventilation rate. Apart from carbon dioxide and carbon monoxide, which must be kept below British Standard 5990 levels of 2,800 and 10 parts per million by volume respectively, sulphur dioxide is the major active contaminant from paraffin and nitrogen oxides from natural gas, bottled gas producing traces of both, with possibly more oxides of nitrogen owing to higher flame temperatures. Nitrogen oxide concentrations are also reported to increase substantially if burners are badly adjusted, particularly with bottled gas. The contaminants may do little harm under normal circumstances, but can exacerbate chemical effects of dampness and condensation. Where there are art works, records, and architectural details of particular value or interest within the church, expert advice should be sought.

A recent introduction from the industrial sector is the direct gas-fired fresh air heater. Fresh air is drawn into the unit, passes over the flame, and the heated air and combustion products are blown into the building together. Mechanical extract and recirculation is used where necessary.

For overall space heating, this is preferable to self-contained flueless heaters since a positive air supply is guaranteed to dilute the products of combustion, and mechanical ventilation without heating is available when required. By introducing fresh air, the RH in the church will normally be reduced, particularly in cold weather. This will help guard against condensation, but the implications of rapid changes in temperature and humidity when the heater is used will need to be reviewed in each instance.

5.5. Local Heating

Where congregations are small, for choir practice and so on, it is unlikely to be economic to heat the whole building, however efficient the system, although some background heating is desirable. People should either be gathered into a smaller enclosed space, such as a side-chapel, or local heating should be considered in the appropriate places, for example the chancel, the pulpit, and the front rows of pews. The aim is to produce the best local radiant temperatures with some local increase in air temperature and a minimum of draughts. Possible techniques include:

> Radiant heating from overhead, using electric or gas units, or possibly an area of heated ceiling. Where the appearance of heaters is unacceptable, infra-red lamps or portable heaters may be appropriate.
>
> Radiant heating from below, using an area of lightweight raised heated floor, or possibly heated floor mats.
>
> Radiant heating from the side, possibly using local heaters in specific locations (e.g. at the lectern). Another possibility is to surround the occupants as far as possible with heated screens which should come down to the floor in order to intercept cold air currents.
>
> In some circumstances, it may be possible to sweep the congregation with a gentle current of warm air from wall or floor grilles or fan assisted heaters.

Where the proportion of the church locally heated is small, and where the use of the local heating is infrequent, the amount of water vapour etc. produced by flueless gas radiant heaters is likely to be of little significance, provided the church is in good condition and inherently dry, and ventilation is adequate.

Box pews assist many local heating arrangements, providing protection from draughts at floor level and concealing heaters, pipes and cables.

FIG. 5.9. PEW HEATING

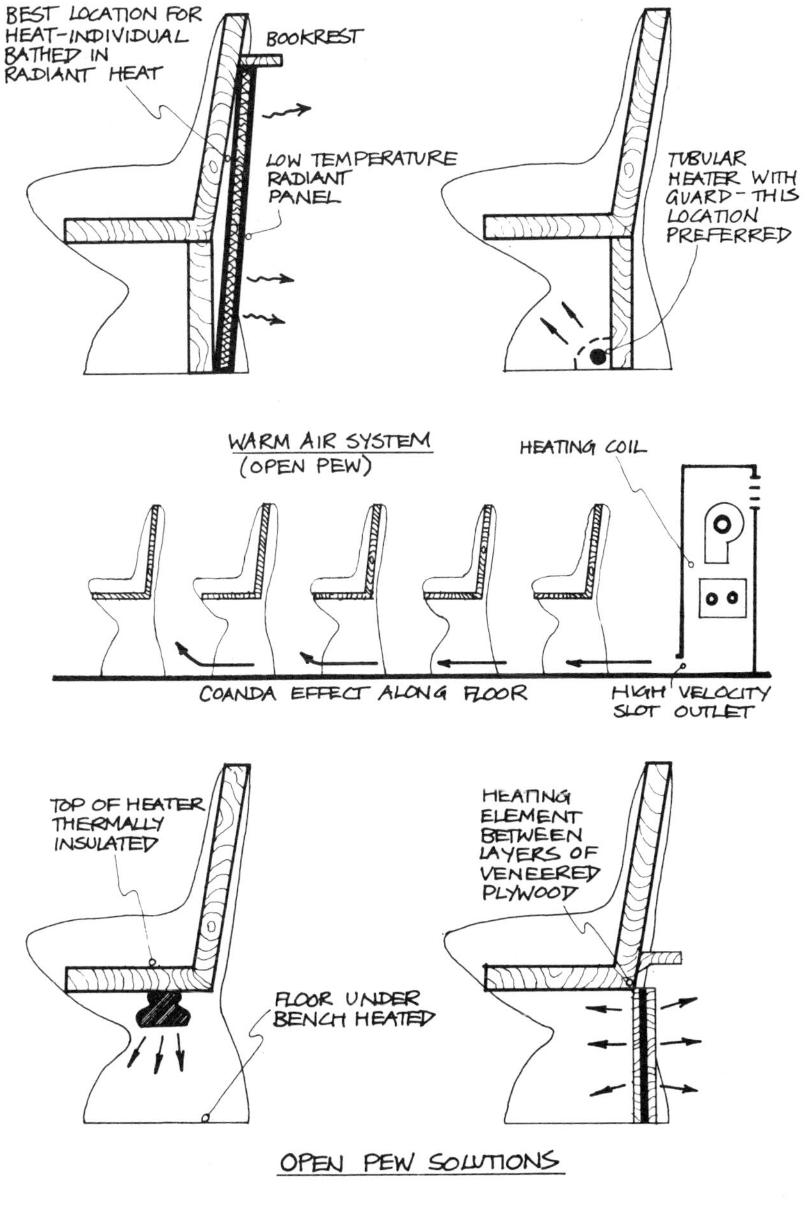

Care must be taken not to damage the pews by the installation or the effects of the heat. Some examples are shown in figure 5.9. Systems work best where they are designed to warm the floor and the congregation as much as possible by radiation; otherwise, feet become cold as the hot air convected from the units is displaced by a cold draught from elsewhere in the church. For economy, electric pew heaters with fast response may be controlled by local interval timers, the occupant of the pew pressing a button to obtain say 30 minutes' heat. Electric heaters must be carefully selected and protected in order to avoid singeing hassocks or burning young children's prying fingers.

6. CENTRAL HEATING

With central heating, heat generated in one place is distributed by means of air, water or steam to local heat emitters. Steam is now little used outside industry, and will not be discussed further. Details of equipment and systems may be found in standard texts.

Central heating originated when coal-firing was universal. It then had the following advantages:

1. Plant and messy coal and ash handling restricted to a single location.
2. Space-consuming and intrusive stoves, fireplaces and flues taken out of the building proper.
3. Higher thermal efficiency than stoves and open fires.
4. Greater controllability than stoves and open fires.
5. Lower capital costs.
6. Lower maintenance costs.
7. Reduced fire risk.

Today, with more alternatives, central heating should not automatically be regarded as the ideal. Reviewing the points above:

1. Central plant is convenient for operation and maintenance, and alterations are possible centrally without affecting the installation elsewhere, giving some flexibility to adapt to changes in fuel availability and price.
2. Modern unit equipment is more compact and less intrusive than its predecessors, though noise levels need checking. Flues, even compact advanced designs, can be difficult to accommodate and a single location will often be preferable.
3. The peak thermal efficiencies of modern unit heaters often differ little from central plant.
4. Controls for all types of heating system are now much improved.
5. Mass-produced and easily-fitted units often cost less installed than the more tailor-made central systems.
6. Central systems are normally longer-lived than units, with fewer parts requiring regular maintenance. However, unit heaters are more simply maintained, parts are standardised and may be kept in stock, and whole units may be replaced individually if necessary.
7. The increased fire risk with unit equipment remains, although substantially mitigated now through improvements in standards of manufacture, design, installation and safety systems.

Central systems often have advantages in safety, longevity, fuel flexibility, and localisation of fuel-burning plant. They are often, however, more expensive to run, particularly with dispersed or occasional heating needs, owing to slow response times, lack of flexibility, and distribution losses. Particular problems arise where:

The system heats a number of spaces simultaneously, often using the same controls, while only some of the spaces are in use. 'Zones' of substantially differing requirements should always have independent time and temperature controls.

When only a small amount of heat is required: in warmer weather, when only a small area is in use, or for domestic hot water, the whole system has to be activated. Even where zone control is good, circulation losses and poor low load boiler efficiencies can often reduce overall thermal efficiencies from 70% or so to 30% or less.

Once there is central heating, it is tempting to use the plant for all heating needs on the site. This made sense where coal-fired plant was fired continuously but with modern equipment it can be inefficient. Unit heaters or even perhaps a small domestic central heating system may be best for other scattered uses. Domestic hot water is a common offender: large tanks and circulating pipework are kept hot (often too hot) for long periods in order to meet an occasional need. Independent hot water systems should always be considered very seriously, even where there is a central system already; if demands are small or infrequent, local electric or gas water heaters can be very cost-effective provided they are manually or automatically switched-off when not required.

6.1. Wet Systems

Systems distributing heat by hot water are of three types: high, medium and low pressure. For reasons of safety and simplicity, however, low pressure hot water (LPHW) systems now predominate. Medium and high pressure systems reduce the size of heat emitters, particularly radiant panels, and older installations may be found. However, they should normally be replaced unless skilled maintenance is available.

In LPHW systems, the water is below atmospheric boiling point and normally leaves the boiler room at about 80° C (180° F), returning at about 70° C (160° F) when the system is warmed-up. For floor heating, and where heat pumps are used, flow temperatures are usually lower, between 40° and 60° C.

Originally, pumps were not readily available and circulation was by gravity. This required large pipes carefully laid out so that the warm water rose away from the boiler. The systems were massive, taking a long time to heat up and for the circulation pattern to be established. They were particularly suitable for coal firing where the boiler seldom went out. The boiler was normally in a basement or underground chamber to improve the circulation head. These chambers often flood, and their suitability for any new equipment should be carefully reviewed.

Today, pumped circulation is universal, although many gravity systems remain, normally with booster (accelerator) pumps added. Pumped circulation allows:

A faster response.

Positive water circulation independent of temperature.

The use of smaller, higher resistance pipes, boilers and heat emitters, simplifying installation and reducing cost.

Great flexibility in boiler location and in pipe layout.

Pumped circulation through existing gravity systems can cause problems. More rapid temperature changes place old pipework and joints under increased thermal stress, which can lead to failure, and sludge may be dislodged, causing blockages.

Circulation systems are of two main types: one-pipe and two-pipe (figure 6.1). Circulation pipes should always be well insulated where they do not provide useful heat directly to the relevant spaces. In the one-pipe system, commonly found in older installations, each radiator returns hot water to the pipe it came from, leading to a temperature drop down the pipe, and requiring radiator sizes to be graded. In the two-pipe system each heat emitter bridges between flow and return pipes, and receives hot water directly from the boiler.

The two-pipe system has become standard for the majority of applications: sizing is simplified and more positive circulation is obtained through each heat emitter. This is particularly important with high efficiency natural and fan convector units, which have small internal waterways and a high hydraulic resistance. Recently, however, the lower installation cost has caused renewed interest in modified one-pipe systems, diverting radiator valves ensuring a positive water flow through each heat emitter when required.

Conventional low pressure hot water systems require a feed and expansion tank above the highest point in the system; this can be difficult to locate in a church and to protect from frost. Small mechanical pressurisation units are now available as an alternative and may be conveniently located in the boiler room (figure 6.1).

Pipes outside the heated space and through which heated water does not circulate (e.g.: water pipes and pipes to feed and expansion vessels) should be well insulated and possibly separately heated by electric heating tape when there is a frost risk.

6.2. Boilers

The heat source for wet systems is known as a boiler, although only in steam systems does the water actually boil. Boilers generally have two parts: the combustion chamber and the convection section where heat is extracted from the gaseous combustion products. Many old boilers and some modern stoves have no convection section at all; their low efficiency is compensated by a long life and few cleaning problems, but the designs date from an age when fuel was cheap.

For fuel economy, it is important to select boilers of high efficiency. Efficiencies are normally quoted at full rated output and until recently were in the range 70–85% of the gross calorific value of the fuel, there being a practical upper limit when water vapour and chemicals from the combustion products condensed and corroded the boiler and flue. Care should be taken in comparing efficiencies as the nett calorific value is sometimes used and gives more impressive-looking figures. Today, condensing boiler designs are being developed, particularly for gas firing, and higher efficiencies are possible.

A boiler which is efficient at full rating is not necessarily efficient on a particular system. Part-load boiler efficiency is usually, although not invariably, worse than that at peak output; system efficiency almost inevitably is, as equipment and distribution systems are kept warm but not fully stretched. Situations where boilers and systems are on light duty should be avoided through design, operation and control. Where they are inevitable, either boilers with good part-load characteristics should be selected, or the load should be split between a number of boilers, with suitable sequence controls (see Chapter 7).

Boilers are generally located in their own rooms, normally to meet regulations, and to reduce problems of noise, safety and intrusion. The boiler room should be adequate in size, dry and not prone to flooding, well-ventilated and with good access; it should be used only for the equipment it contains, and not as a dump. If these requirements are

FIG. 6.1. HOT WATER CENTRAL HEATING SCHEMATICS

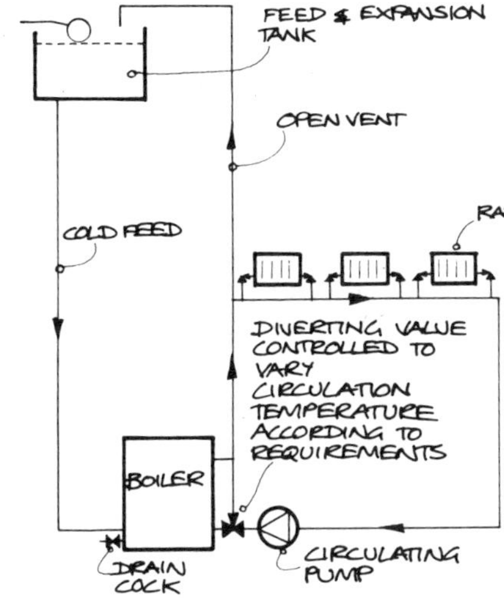

ONE-PIPE SYSTEM ALSO ILLUSTRATING COMPENSATED TEMPERATURE CIRCULATION AND CONVENTIONAL FEED AND EXPANSION TANK

TWO-PIPE SYSTEM ALSO ILLUSTRATING CONSTANT TEMPERATURE CIRCULATION AND PRESSURIZATION UNIT

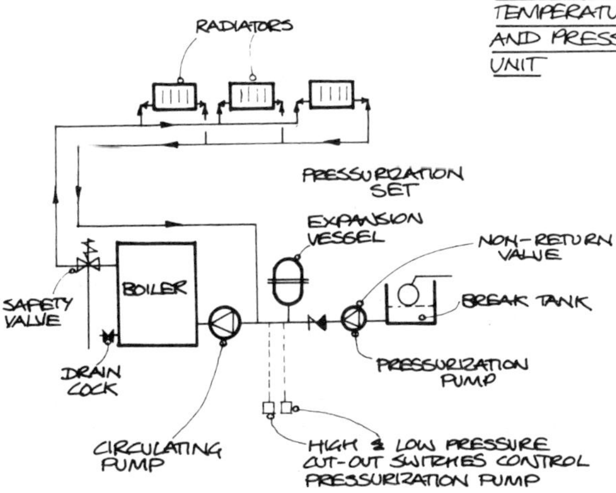

ignored (and they often are!) the result will be poor maintenance, reduced life and efficiency, and increased safety and fire hazards.

The traditional heating boiler, assembled from cast iron sections, is relatively large and heavy. Suitable locations are restricted; if foundations are not sound the castings may crack. Although often quite efficient under sustained full and part-loads, their mass and large water content gives them a slow thermal response which makes them best suited to continuous heating applications.

Most boilers are now fabricated from steel, copper or light iron castings: they are generally more compact and convenient generally. Peak efficiencies are similar to well-designed and maintained sectional boilers, and on a year-round basis efficiencies are often higher, owing to faster response to demand. The life of fabricated boilers, between 10 and 20 years, is generally less than sectional ones, but this is often compensated by lower purchase, installation and running costs. The units are however more likely to fail if system design or operation is faulty. Infrequent operation does not necessarily prolong boiler life, since damage is caused by thermal stresses, condensation and corrosion.

In commercial and industrial installations, it is common to split the load between two or more boilers; this provides standby capacity for maintenance and breakdown, and gives a better load match between boiler output and heating demand in milder weather. This duplication will probably be extravagant in the smaller and intermittently-heated church, but is worthwhile for the larger and more continuously operated installation. A more recent development is the use of a larger number of identical small modular gas or oil boilers. These can simplify installation where space is restricted, and allow improved fuel efficiencies at part loads, provided they are properly controlled.

Interest is growing in hot water central heating systems which use more than one heat source. For example:

1. A small coal boiler meets the background and mild weather heating requirement efficiently, with a simple and regular operating procedure. When more heat is required, a supplementary gas or oil-fired boiler is brought in.
2. A heat pump meets the background and mild weather heating requirement. In colder weather, a boiler is used either as an alternative or, with some sophistication in design, as a supplement.

3. An oil-fired system is efficient but expensive to run. An electric boiler is added to the circuit and is used to preheat the building during the small hours using off-peak electricity. When the off-peak tariff ceases, the oil boiler is brought on.

These methods are only likely to be practical and cost-effective for sustained heating demands, though electric preheating may have wider applications.

6.3. District or Group Heating

Occasionally hot water will be available from site mains serving an area or a group of buildings. Rates for heat supply may be competitive, particularly when the need not to purchase, operate and maintain boilers is taken into account. Nevertheless, this type of system is best suited to more continuous heating needs, and the prospect of potentially cheap heat should not override other considerations in system selection. In principle, it is important that all users of communal heating are metered and charged for what they use; otherwise there is little incentive to conserve and hence higher apportioned charges for all. Sometimes, however, churches are offered very low flat rates which it would be silly to refuse provided the contract runs for a reasonable time.

6.4. Re-Use of Old Systems

Old hot water heating systems may often be in a sound condition, with the exception of the boiler, pump and control: should they be replaced? The answer depends largely on how effective they were in the first place, and whether it is desirable to retain a hot water system as background or full central heating.

If the answer is yes, or probably yes, to both questions, the system should be checked in detail. This would involve:

A visual inspection of all heat emitters and pipework.

Pressure test of the system.

Draining down and chemical test of water in the system.

Removal and inspection of typical lengths of pipework.

If these tests were satisfactory, the system would need to be thoroughly flushed out, cleaned externally, and have any defective parts replaced. Specialist advice should be obtained on suitable chemical treatment for the water in the system: this applies to newer systems as well. Alterations to the existing system should otherwise be kept to a minimum, as they may disturb otherwise sound parts of the installation; if more heat emitters are required, they should normally be on a separate circuit. The boiler size will also need review to ensure sufficient capacity. Any heat emitters added to the original circuit should have large waterways similar to the originals. Modern high-efficiency natural and fan convectors will not obtain sufficient circulation and some types may be prone to blockage if any remaining sludge is dislodged, as may the waterways in modern low water content boilers; strainers are advisable.

Most of the older systems will have been designed for continuous coal firing and lower internal temperatures than today: their large water content and limited heating surface thus makes them slow-responding and generally unsuitable for occasional heating needs. Large diameter cast iron pipes with caulked joints are often found: although they may have lasted for nearly a century, modern pumps and boilers may subject them to rapid temperature fluctuations which can cause leaks and cracks. Older systems are therefore most appropriate for background heating, coupled to a small boiler or possibly a heat pump; with low circulating water temperatures the boiler should have a by-pass to protect it from sustained condensation, or a suitable high efficiency condensing boiler may be specified.

The large water content in an older system not only slows down warm-up times but is also a substantial reservoir of heat. Controls should be arranged to allow the boiler to cease firing well before the end of the timed period while the pump continues running to allow the stored heat to be dissipated into the building.

6.5. Warm Air Systems

Warm air systems are less common in the UK in general and in churches in particular. The size of ducts required and the location requirements for diffusers generally restricts sensitive applications to new buildings and to major alteration works. Careful design is required to control noise levels.

Forced air systems use an air heat exchanger in place of the waterways in a boiler and a fan in place of the pump. Sometimes flueless firing is used. Fuel-burning air heaters should preferably be in fire resistant compartments (for larger units they may be statutorily necessary), and ductwork requires fire dampers where it passes between compartments. In order to reduce duct sizes a number of heaters are often used; these may alternatively have hot water heating coils, supplied from a central boiler plant, which increases controllability and reduces noise problems and fire risks. Good frost protection arrangements for fresh air heater coils are vital.

FIG. 6.2. WARM AIR SYSTEMS SECTIONS

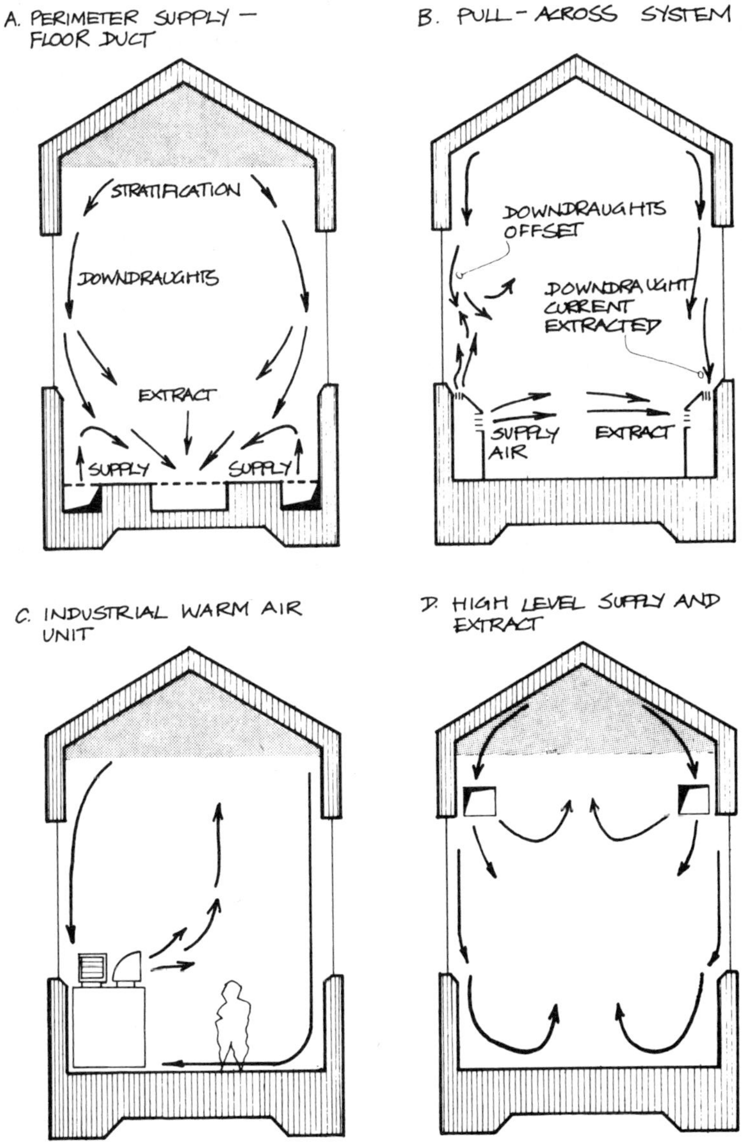

As with water systems, the earlier types used gravity circulation by natural buoyancy, while today forced fan-assisted circulation is standard. Gravity systems are sometimes found, often with hot air stoves in pits under the floor: they usually cause draughts, stains, and bad stratification, and are best replaced. Flues can have long horizontal runs and may be unsafe, particularly where intermittent use no longer allows a good draught to be established. It may be possible to use the ducts as part of a new hot water or forced warm air system.

Forced air systems in churches are often poor, with single unit heater blasting out hot air noisily and indiscriminately. Good systems are also possible, especially in new buildings, where air is carefully diffused throughout the church to give a fast warm-up, good temperature distribution and to avoid draughts and stratification. Figure 6.2 illustrates a few typical sectional arrangements; these are not intended to be definitive, but merely to show the care required if draughts and stratification are to be avoided.

Air flow in ducted systems has to be carefully balanced between the outlets to ensure effective heat distribution. Ductwork should be leak-tight and insulated. Where fresh air is introduced through the system the volume and any controls need to be carefully set up: too much outside air will lead to dryness and high fuel use, too little could result in high relative humidities.

7. AUTOMATIC CONTROLS

Accurate control is essential both for efficient energy use and to get the best results from limited heating budgets. Control technology is currently advancing rapidly, and this discussion is therefore rather general. A number of devices and methods discussed are seldom found in churches today but new electronic equipment is becoming competitive.

Controls are the vital connection between the user and the system; they should be correctly located, simple to operate and easy to understand. Many control systems, excellent in all other respects, are ineffective owing to a lack of appreciation of the way in which they will be used. A time switch is unlikely to be set sensibly if it is in a locked metal cabinet full of mysterious electrical equipment in a dirty subterranean boiler chamber. Equally, nothing is entirely automatic, successful operation ultimately relies on someone checking and making adjustments to match the performance of the system most economically to the requirements.

For convenience, controls are considered in five groups: safety, time, capacity, temperature, and humidity and ventilation.

7.1. Safety Controls

Safety controls are essential to avoid danger if systems fail in some way, particularly through overheating, escape of unburnt fuel, or failure of electrical equipment. Safety devices are normally supplied as an integral part of 'packaged' boilers and heaters. They will include a high temperature cut-out, a flame failure device where appropriate, and interlocks between logically connected operations (e.g.: fan to run before fuel can be supplied to a forced draught burner).

Church heating will often operate when there is nobody present, or even close by, and additional protection will usually be necessary. For instance:

Some high temperature cut-outs reset automatically; this is not advisable since faults may persist undetected.

In hot water central heating systems, a flow switch should be fitted to stop the boiler firing if water flow is interrupted; this is essential for low water content boilers. Warm air units should also have a similar device in the air stream.

A fusible link and gravity fire valve should be considered as a final fail-safe on high rated equipment, even where not statutorily necessary (e.g: for gas boilers). If possible, the fire valve should be at the fuel tank outlet or the point of entry to the boiler room, with a clearly identified quick-release at the door.

Boilers should also be equipped with a safety valve, a pressure gauge, and thermometers for flow, return and flue gas temperatures. Further safety devices and controls may be fitted if the situation is thought to merit them. For instance, a float switch may be fitted in a tank (e.g.: a water feed and expansion tank) to isolate the system and sound an alarm if the water level is low. The correct operation of these devices should be checked regularly.

Wet central heating systems need to be protected from frost regardless of all other control settings.

The simplest method uses a carefully-placed and accurate (preferably electronic or mercury) room thermostat to start the system if the internal temperature falls below say 5°C. Some modern equipment uses the same sensor for room temperature control and for frost protection. The more common and cheaper bimetallic thermostats are generally less precise, and unless set high (when they may bring the heating on unnecessarily) they might not protect the system reliably.

Preferably, an accurate external thermostat, commonly known as a frost stat, may be used. This may be set to a lower temperature, practically at 2 or 3°C to compensate for any inaccuracy. A room thermostat at a low frost setting should be installed as well to avoid unnecessarily long running hours.

For churches which are heated regularly, the frost stat may be used to start the circulating pumps only. If the return water temperature then falls below a low pre-set limit, the boiler is fired. Care must be taken to avoid prolonged condensation within the boiler from long periods of intermittent firing at low circulating temperatures.

Frost protection systems should be checked from time to time, to make sure that they work and also that they do not bring the heating on needlessly when there is no freezing risk. A maximum and minimum thermometer in the church is a useful check.

7.2. Time Controls

All systems will benefit from time controls, if only to switch everything on and off as necessary. More elaborate versions can programme equipment, space and circulation temperatures for different periods. The selection and location of time controls requires a degree of care and thought which, sadly, it seldom receives. For instance, many churches have domestic time switches designed to repeat the same programme every 24 hours. A common form of commercial timer allows whole days (e.g: Monday to Saturday) to be omitted from the programme, but it is difficult to set and not particularly well suited to varying uses and heating needs during the week. A daily programme also does not permit extended warm up times when necessary. The result is that although the heating could have come on at, say, 11 p.m. on Saturday evening, it is switched on earlier manually at the convenience of the person responsible. Many time controls are also inconveniently located, difficult to see, and difficult to set, and are thus incorrectly used or bypassed altogether. Clock hands or a digital time display are useful aids to correct setting.

A 7-day time switch is normally the simplest appropriate type. The settings can be changed at any time, but frequently it will be convenient to establish a routine. Some time switches can cover an entire month's programme, but they either have very coarse control settings or are expensive and more difficult to set than the 7-day units.

Electronic time controls are also available. These permit more accurate and sophisticated programming than an electromechanical time switch, and can often programme a number of devices from the one unit. With some products, a programme may be established for the entire year, taking account of events at regular weekly, monthly or quarterly intervals, and also 'forgetting' ad hoc instructions after they have been executed. This sounds ideal, but they require skill to set up and the programme is not normally displayed all at once: the unit has to be 'interrogated', a process which many people find irritating and confusing.

Units with automatic clockwork or battery reserves should be specified to avoid the need to reset every time the electrical supply is interrupted. An extended reserve period with a fast recovery time may be required where the electricity is habitually switched off when the church is not in use. However, switching-off supplies to heating controls is not recommended, particularly for wet systems where frost protection facilities are lost; electrical distribution boards and isolating switches should be arranged accordingly.

Since the warm-up time of a building varies with outside temperature, sun and wind conditions, and the internal starting temperature, fixed time controls are not ideal, especially for slow-responding systems and buildings. Equally, the thermal capacity of a massive building may allow heat to be switched off before occupancy ceases. Optimum start/stop controls do this automatically and are worth considering, particularly for wet central heating systems in regular intermittent use.

The optimum start process is outlined in figure 7.1. The controller requires internal and external temperature sensors and is set much as a time switch, but only to the periods during which the church will actually be occupied. It then calculates the necessary warm-up time and starts the system accordingly. Some units require calibration by the installer; others monitor the building's warm-up characteristics and calibrate themselves. A simplified form of this control uses an outside thermostat to bring the heating on late or not at all when outside temperatures are high. Optimum start gives improved performance and saves heating fuel in mild weather, but when it is cold, the heating may run for longer. In order to avoid excessive preheat periods, the earliest allowable start time may be entered on most units. Performance should be checked from time to time, to see that running hours are as expected – some controllers can show the time at which they started the heating, and when they intend to stop it.

With many wet heating systems, particularly the older ones with 4-inch pipes and cast-iron boilers, much heat is stored bringing the boiler and distribution pipework up to temperature. The boiler should thus be turned-off before the end of the heating period, while the pump continues running to dissipate this stored heat effectively into the building. This is normally achieved by either a 'run-on' timer on the pump or a reverse-acting thermostat on the boiler flow pipe, which keeps the pump running until the temperature has dropped to a pre-set level.

Time controls should be located in a convenient position, but where they cannot be interfered with by unauthorised people. A locked box by the door or the wall in the vestry are often suitable. Before selecting any particular control one should make sure that the person who will adjust it understands it and considers it convenient to use. Controls requiring regular adjustment should not normally be put inside equipment control panels, as this makes people frightened to use them. Unforeseen heating requrements will arise outside the normal programme, and a manual override is convenient, preferably to operate the system for a predetermined interval and then return to normal automatically.

7.3. Capacity Controls

Capacity controls regulate heat input or output in accordance with estimated requirements. The most common types are input controllers, sequence controllers and compensated controllers.

FIG. 7.1. OPTIMUM START CONTROL

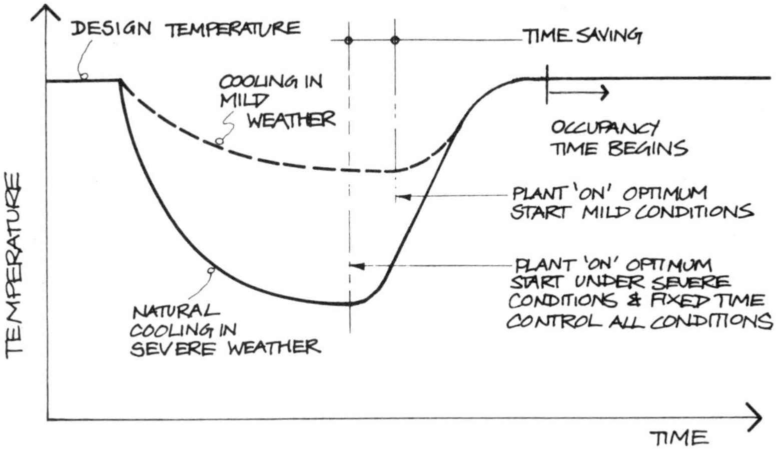

FIG. 7.2. HEATING S–CURVE FOR A TYPICAL BOILER SYSTEM

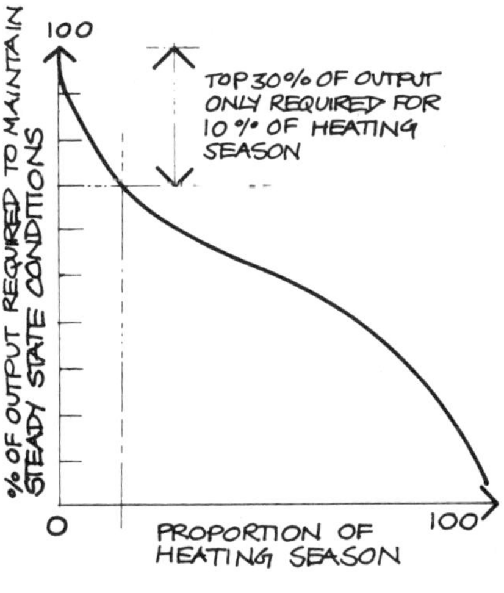

FIG. 7.3. TYPICAL COMPENSATED CONTROL

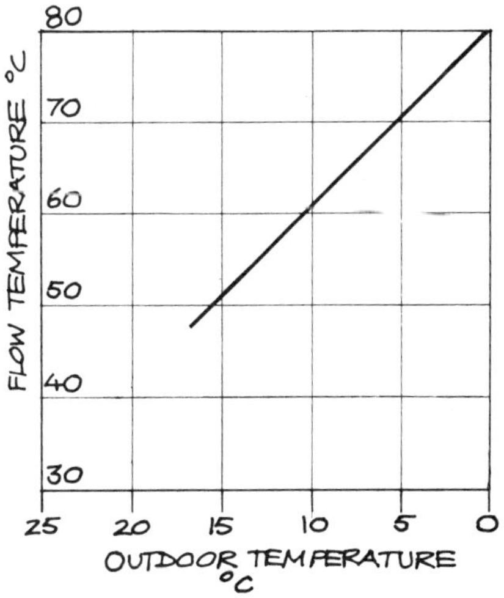

Input Controllers are used with heat storage systems, such as electric night storage heaters and floor heating, to avoid too much heat being put into store: they are particularly necessary with intermittent use, since any excess will be lost when nobody is there. The simplest controller relates the charge merely to the prevailing external temperature; more sophisticated ones take account of the inside temperature and of the period over which heat is required for the coming day.

Sequence Controllers Many boilers are most efficient when operating continuously at full output. They are sized, however, to meet a peak requirement which obtains for only a small part of the year (figure 7.2). During milder weather it may be best to restrict the number of boilers or heaters in operation. Manual sequencing is normally sufficient, but for a larger building in more frequent use automatic sequence control may be considered.

Compensated Controllers (figure 7.3) It is often useful to control the maximum available output from wet central heating by altering the circulating water temperature by means of a 'compensator'. Simple compensators schedule circulation temperatures in accordance with outside temperature while more sophisticated units also take into account internal temperatures and occasionally sun and wind conditions. Compensated control is particularly useful with hot water radiators and radiant convectors; it should not normally be applied to forced air and fan convector systems or draughts will result, and it does not work as well where different types of heat emitter are used on the same water circuit. It is best if the compensation is overridden while the building is warming up. Otherwise, lower circulation temperatures in mild weather will extend the pre-heat period unnecessarily.

7.4. Temperature Controls

Many church heating systems are only operated in extremis and space temperature limiting control may appear ludicrous. Nevertheless, overheating and excess running times commonly occur, particularly in milder weather.

Warm air and fan convector heaters often have integral controls which detect the temperature of room air returning to the unit; these are often limited in accuracy and it is difficult to achieve consistency between settings. Central or group control is often preferable. Fan convectors can usefully be controlled by two thermostats to run them at high speed for warm-up and to drop to the quieter low speed as the required temperature is approached.

Thermostatic radiator valves are an effective low-cost method of controlling hot water radiators and convectors, but they are not normally suitable for existing one-pipe systems. The sensing heads should be installed where they are not affected by heat from the emitters or from the connecting pipework; valves with remote sensors or setting dials may be used where necessary. The valves are particularly useful for heaters in smaller rooms attached to a central system. Setting heads with robust tamperproof guards should normally be specified to avoid damage and unauthorised adjustment. Where local adjustment is required, a click-stop at the preferred position gives a useful reminder and makes re-setting easy.

Some hot water convectors are controlled by dampers in the air stream. These are often rather crude and ineffective and thermostatically-operated valves on the water side are preferable.

Domestic room thermostats with open dials and bimetallic or capsule elements are often used in churches. However:

Tamperproof versions should normally be selected.

The cheaper versions can have a wide temperature differential between switching-off and coming-on which causes discomfort and energy waste, particularly with warm air heating.

Where accelerator heaters are fitted to speed up response times, a fixed setting gives higher air temperatures in mild weather than when it is colder, while the opposite behaviour would be more comfortable and economical.

High accuracy electronic or mercury temperature sensors, although more expensive, should be seriously considered, particularly for large areas and for frost protection. Adjustment should be easy but tampering should be discouraged; with electronic controls the dial may be separate from the sensor, perhaps beside the time controls. Some products may be programmed to achieve different space temperatures for different time periods.

It can be difficult to choose a good location for a temperature sensor or thermostat. On an outside wall, it is affected by heat loss and thermal capacity of the structure, while beneath a window it may suffer from downdraughts or heat rising from pipes below. A good place is often on a lightweight screen or furnishing away from windows and heat emitters. In a larger installation, a number of detectors may be installed and suitable combinations employed; for instance, controlling from the maximum, minimum or average of a number of readings.

With radiant heating it is possible to use thermostats which respond to both radiant and air temperatures. Location of these sensors is critical and should be discussed carefully with manufacturers and designers.

With central heating systems, compensated controls may be supplemented with room thermostats and thermostatic radiator valves to avoid local overheating. When a number of spaces (e.g. a church and church hall) are heated by the same installation, independent time and temperature controls for each space are essential. These would generally open a motorised valve to the zone when heat is required and only energise the boiler when one or more of the valves was open.

7.5. Humidity and Ventilation Controls

Automatic control of humidity and ventilation in a church is not common, but should be thought about.

> Where humidity can build up to dangerous levels, ventilation or possibly dehumidification may be controlled to remove it. Control could be either by time, internal relative humidities or by moisture levels in vulnerable building elements.
>
> In order to benefit from the heat storage capacity of a massive church building, ventilation may be organised when the external temperature is in excess of that inside, provided that condensation would not result.

Most humidity sensors require recalibration at regular intervals, and at least an annual check. However, some types are increasing in reliability and are likely to become used more widely.

7.6. Adjustment and Commissioning

Controls cannot be expected to achieve exactly what they purport to do. A simple example is a thermostat: the temperature about which it controls is unlikely to be what the dial says: the actual room temperature needs to be checked from time to time with a good thermometer, and an estimate of resultant temperature may be required. A wet-and-dry bulb hygrometer is best purchased and used strictly in accordance with instructions; this will also give a useful check on relative humidities.

It is unwise to assume that controls will function faultlessly the first time: it is all too common for them to be connected incorrectly if at all! Proving tests should be specified and witnessed by a client representative and the results recorded. On the larger and more complex systems the appointment of an independent commissioning engineer should be seriously considered.

8. SYSTEM SELECTION AND INSTALLATION

It is all too easy to make a poor choice when installing or replacing heating because the needs and requirements appear obvious. The boiler is elderly or broken down: clearly it should be replaced; the church is cold: clearly more heat is required; the heating costs too much to run: clearly the church needs to be insulated and draughtproofed, the hours of heating operation restricted, and a cheaper fuel used; a new church is being built: clearly it should be well centrally heated (clients often give little priority to reducing running costs until they get the first fuel bills). As we have seen above, however, the problems and solutions are often more complex than this. If the existing heating system, or parts of it, are in reasonable condition, it may be possible to enhance its performance significantly by improving efficiency, upgrading controls, or adding a few more heat emitters. Possibilities are dealt with in the next chapter; here we are more concerned with new systems, or with the replacement or major upgrading of existing ones.

8.1. Stating the Requirements

A clear brief should be set down which will often need to incorporate requirements for preservation, ventilation and humidity control in addition to the heating itself. Specialist advice will often be required to prepare the brief: heating consultants and contractors cannot be expected to know about special features of the building and its contents which might be indirectly affected for better or worse by the heating. The specialists should also be asked to comment on the proposals.

The brief should state:

The areas to be included in the project, with typical uses, times of use, and the comfort conditions required during those times, at given outside design conditions.

Any temperature, humidity and air quality requirements necessary for the preservation of the building and its contents.

Physical and aesthetic constraints on the installation.

Any relevant technical requirements and standards.

Where appropriate, any requirements for investigating the re-use of the existing system.

General intentions regarding operation, control and maintenance.

The relative importance of capital and running costs and the criteria under which additional investment to reduce running cost might be considered.

Any requirements for future flexibility in extent of system, patterns of use, furnishing arrangements, and fuel choice.

Procedures to be followed and safeguards required during the installation work.

The brief should also include relevant background information (e.g. plans, sections, specifications, mechanical and electrical drawings, main supply capacities, studies previously undertaken), or at least a guide to what exists and where it can be found.

The brief should be widely discussed in order to reach a balanced view and to make sure that all concerned appreciate what is to be done. Otherwise too much may be expected: living room conditions with the stability of a museum at minimum running cost!

8.2. The Heating Consultant

Clients may be tempted to rely on the expertise of heating suppliers and installers and save the cost of a heating consultant. This may sometimes be appropriate if the requirements are clear, simple, and specific. Without a brief, however, it can be impossible to judge between apples and oranges in different suppliers' speculative schemes. Installers and suppliers are also likely to make their choice from a limited range of equipment, and their concern will normally be to provide a cost-effective installation which meets specified temperature standards, and not necessarily about things such as minimum running cost, intelligibility to the user, flexibility in operation, and response to future change. Unless encouraged, there is also little incentive to attend to finer details, which may improve performance and appearance but by adding to the tender price may lose them the job. A few unscrupulous salesmen even browbeat vicars into the purchase of equipment on the basis of claimed fuel cost savings and wave away legitimate concerns about possible adverse effects.

A heating consultant is therefore recommended, preferably for a full design and contract supervision service but at least to help define the problems, review statutory and insurance requirements, establish a performance specification, and comment on contractors' proposals and workmanship. Names may be obtained from the appropriate Institutions. In order to benefit from feedback it will often be best to identify suitable individuals or firms in an area and to retain them for advice on a number of churches over a period.

8.3. System Selection

The selection needs to be made carefully by the client, in conjunction with his architect and heating consultant. Some of the rules have been established in the preceding chapters and will not be repeated here. Difficult decisions will often need to be made, and should not be assigned to those who may not see the whole picture. Before a scheme is finalised, it should be discussed carefully with those who will operate and maintain it, who will often have valuable insights into details of design, specification, installation and operation.

Although each building and its requirements must be considered individually, certain situations recur. Solutions depend very much on the size of the church, its intensity of use and whether other facilities are combined with it, fuel availability and cost. Simply, in an occasionally used church, one does not want to waste a lot of heat warming the fabric excessively, and radiant and air heating will be the most effective. With more continuous use, the fabric will inevitably be warmed and so there is a wider range of heating options, though one should avoid circumstances with high temperatures and too much ventilation, which may lead to excessive dryness in winter.

Whatever the size and occupancy, it is vital that the heating and ventilation are also arranged to protect the church and its contents as far as possible from decay; anything else will only bring forward the day when expensive repairs are required. Normally, the requirements are to arrange for adequate ventilation or dehumidification to avoid sustained condensation and remove excess moisture, and for sufficient heating to keep all vulnerable surfaces above the dew point temperature of the air. Closer control may be necessary where there are valuable items to be preserved.

In many situations, whether or not the existing heating promotes decay depends on the associated ventilation. It will often be enough to ensure a small through-draught at all times and to make someone responsible for opening a larger number of ventilators once a week, preferably following the most intensive period of occupancy. In fine, dry weather the building can be further warmed and excess moisture removed by leaving the doors and windows open for longer periods, but not overnight when the temperature falls and the relative humidity rises.

To determine whether ventilation rates are appropriate a thermohygrograph should be placed in the church and the degree and method of ventilation varied; it should soon become clear what is having a significant effect on relative humidities.

If it is difficult to find people to adjust the ventilation, then automatic control of mechanical ventilation or dehumidification should be seriously considered. The effectiveness of these will normally be greater and the overall cost less than the consequences of either ignoring the problem or attempting to solve it by heating alone.

8.4. Some Installation Requirements

Associated builders' work may cost as much as the heating itself, and the choice of system will often be influenced by the need to keep it to a minimum. Great care is required, something which firms and operatives without long experience of church work may not appreciate.

In order to minimise disruption and possible damage, good use should be made of existing facilities (such as Victorian floor ducts) in a new installation, and any cutting into the building should be minimised. A badly-located item can always be repositioned; something wrongly cut-out may be lost for ever. Any boring or cutting-out should always be carefully set out in advance, under architectural supervision, and the work done by the appropriate craftsman and not by the pipe fitter. The progress of all cutting should be carefully monitored: for instance, walls thought to be solid may turn out to be rubble-filled and could be seriously weakened. Small test holes should be made first if there is any uncertainty. Permissible drilling and cutting techniques should be carefully specified: modern vibratory tools can weaken the structure and loose materials may fall away.

In historic buildings, the following guidelines should always be followed:

Chases should not be made in brickwork, masonry or plaster without the consent of the architect.

Holes or chases should not be made in or through buttresses, piers, mullions, columns, detached shafts or vaulting ribs without the consent of the architect.

No holes should be drilled in, or fixings made to bosses, unless they have already been drilled for a previous installation.

Pipes should not be laid over the surface of carvings, paintings or mouldings.

Holes should be as small as possible, carefully drilled and inconspicuously located.

All brackets and fixings should be as small as practicable.

Moisture and corrosion-resistant materials should always be used for exterior work, and preferably throughout.

Before any work is started, the heating contractor should submit proposals for the routes of all pipes and cables and the precise locations of all items of equipment. Typical details of holes and fixings should also be submitted, with samples where necessary. All routes and positions and any alterations to the drawn scheme should be agreed on site before any work commences.

Heaters and pipework should be selected and located to avoid staining surfaces and decorations. The following guidelines should be followed:

Radiators and other high temperature heat sources fixed close to walls cause bad stains. A projecting shelf above helps but to be effective it must also project at least 150 mm at either side, turn down a similar amount at the ends and be well sealed to the wall at the back.

Natural convectors with top discharge give similar problems. Front discharge units and skirting convectors are preferable, or the units should be spaced 100 mm or more away from the wall. Convectors and heaters against walls should be sealed at the back, or to a flat backing board if the wall is uneven.

Fan convectors and forced warm air systems give little trouble except where wall grilles are set flush and the system remains warm while the fan is off. Grilles should be well sealed round the edge or streaks may appear. Flush grilles should never be used with gravity warm air systems as they cause bad stains.

Pipes and electric tubular heaters cause troublesome staining if less than about 40 mm from the wall and at brackets; floor stands are best, otherwise insulated brackets should be used or the pipes encased.

Pattern staining may occur where some parts of a surface are colder than others, as with plaster ceilings on wooden joists. The effect is particularly noticeable where the surface is swept by air currents from convector heaters and large column radiators. The problem may be cured by insulation above or by using different heaters.

It is essential to obtain as-fitted drawings of the system, (preferably with a framed schematic fixed to the wall), a record of all items of equipment and their maintenance requirements, commissioning records, and clear operating and maintenance instructions for the entire system. There should also be simple instructions on the use of the controls and records of their preferred settings, and a fault-finding procedure for the non-specialist. It can be difficult to get satisfactory material from the contractors, and assistance from the architect and the heating consultant will often be necessary to ensure that the information is of the right quality, and that any consequential problems which might arise from incorrect use of the system are identified where possible. Three copies should normally be requested, one for filing, one to be available within the church, and one to be stored in the church safe, in case the others become lost.

8.5. Flues and Chimneys

Flues often give technical and aesthetic problems. They need to be matched to the appliance and to comply with Building Regulations and the Clean Air Act. However, where an old system is replaced by one of equivalent power, detailed compliance with current Acts may not be necessary.

Larger boilers require substantial flues which can be difficult to accommodate. Existing flues will not necessarily be suitable, since:

The path may be tortuous; it may have relied on continuous heat from a coal-fired appliance to work satisfactorily.

The lining will often have failed.

The area may be inadequate for more powerful equipment.

Condensation of water vapour and combustion products from gas and oil may damage the flue.

Where flue gas temperatures are increased, the flue may fail and ignite nearby timbers or inflammable materials deposited in the roof space by birds, for example.

Satisfactory cleaning arrangements may be difficult to organise.

The re-use of an existing flue requires a thorough survey. Sharp bends may have to be eased, and replacement of re-lining may be necessary. For gas equipment only, it may be possible to use a flexible stainless steel flue liner. A properly-lined flue of insufficient capacity for atmospheric combustion may be adequate for pressurised burners, or with fan assistance. Older flues usually have a large thermal capacity and may not function correctly under natural draught until thoroughly warm; this may never occur if heating operates intermittently, exacerbating condensation and sooting problems. Where flues are not suitably lined, particularly for gas boilers, chemicals from the previous oil and coal combustion may work through to the face, damaging masonry and plasterwork. Prefabricated insulated flues, often in stainless steel, are now widely used for new installations. Balanced and dilution flues for gas and some small oil boilers have been discussed earlier.

9. GETTING THE BEST OUT OF HEATING SYSTEMS

This last chapter is concerned with operating and maintaining existing and new systems to give the best performance with minimum fuel use. It also deals with relatively low cost methods of upgrading existing installations. Although it is commonly felt that churches cost too much to heat, in relation to their volume much less is normally spent than on other building types. The problem of getting maximum benefit for minimum outlay is nevertheless very real.

9.1. Operation and Maintenance

Too often heating systems are taken for granted until they go wrong. The result is that equipment goes out of tune and develops undetected faults, control settings become inappropriate, performance deteriorates and fuel consumption increases. When faults finally become apparent, some damage has often been done and repair costs more than it should.

There is really no alternative to making somebody who is interested, capable, and committed responsible for the operation and maintenance of the system, and for monitoring its fuel consumption. This does not mean he has to carry out technical inspections and clean the burners himself, but a maintenance contractor is unlikely to keep up to the mark if nobody keeps an eye on his work, draws attention to shortcomings, checks his bills, and thanks him when the job has been well done. Contractors also cannot be expected to know as much about the detailed pattern of use of the church and the perceived performance of the heating as those who use the church regularly; nor can they easily judge the required balance between comfort and the associated fuel costs, and they will be inclined to set controls generously to avoid call-backs.

The duties of the person responsible should include:

Having a full knowledge of any heating, ventilation and humidity control systems.

Being aware of the way in which the systems can be made to operate most effectively, particularly through switching equipment off entirely at times when it is unlikely to be needed.

Knowing the detailed pattern of use of the church and making sure that the controls are set to meet the comfort requirements effectively, but without waste.

Checking the operation of the system (e.g. time switching, value operation, flame characteristics, circulation and flue gas temperatures) from time to time to make sure that all is well.

Monitoring space temperatures and humidities from time to time to check the performance of the system (it may be possible to reduce thermostat and time settings, particularly in milder weather), and to be aware of possible dangers to the building fabric and its contents.

Arranging for maintenance, and checking that it has been properly carried out.

In order to assist the person in his duties, controls should be conveniently located and well laid out, as previously discussed. Monitoring devices should also be available, particularly:

A maximum and minimum thermometer.

A simple hygrometer.

For central heating boilers and the larger air heaters, thermometers showing flow, return and flue gas temperatures.

A wet and dry bulb whirling hygrometer is also useful for more accurate spot checks. Where problems are detected, more sophisticated recording equipment (such as a thermohygrograph or its electronic equivalent) may be borrowed or hired, and it is hoped that suitable monitoring services will be more widely available to churches in the future.

Arrangements should be made for boilers, burners, flues, pumps, fans and controls to be thoroughly checked at least once a year and heat emitters cleaned from time to time. Chemical tests and water treatment may also be necessary. The work needs to be carefully specified and supervised. Combustion efficiency tests and burner adjustments should be made regularly, particularly with oil and forced draught gas burners. Chimney cleaning should not be forgotten, particularly with solid fuel equipment; where wood and waste products are burned, this may be several times a year.

9.2. Monitoring Fuel Consumption

Many consumers greet their fuel costs with resigned acceptance. When the bills come, or when the accounts are made up, it is too late to do much; one can only pray that things will be better next season. However, excess fuel consumption is a useful symptom of something wrong: a faulty control, poor burner adjustment, ventilators left open, or a time switch or thermostat changed to meet some unusual requirement and not re-set. Once a review procedure is established, monitoring fuel use against targets is a quick, simple and effective method of managing fuel expenditure and ensuring optimum plant performance.

FIG. 9.1. FUEL CONSUMPTION

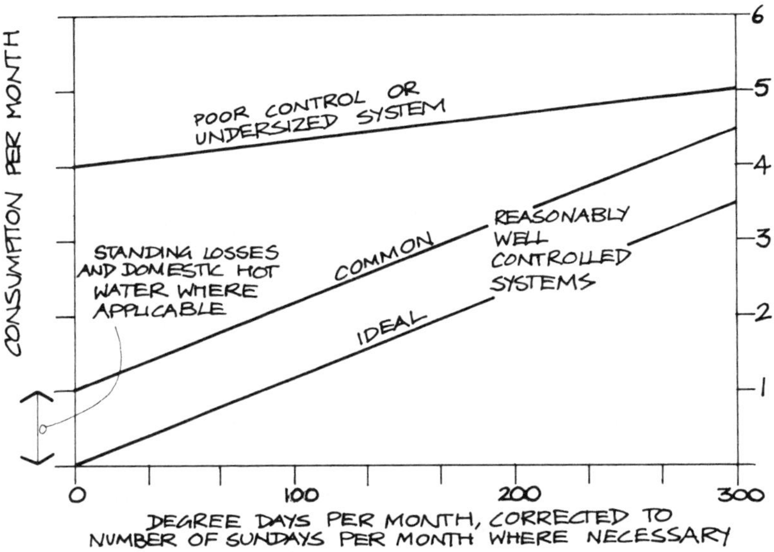

Records are usually kept of the cost of fuel used, but not the amount. Meter readings should be taken preferably at weekly and certainly at monthly intervals: a quarterly bill is too long after the event. With stored fuel such as oil, delivery records are a poor indication of the fuel burned; more exact measurement is best, preferably by meter which also helps to avoid fraud.

Where main gas and electricity meters supply a number of locations, sub-meters on the supplies to the church are desirable. An hour-run meter on the burner circuit is also a worthwhile check on the intensity of use.

Plant performance may be reviewed by plotting the fuel used each month against average outside temperature or degree days (regional figures are available from the Department of Energy and local figures may often be obtained from the Meteorological Office, airports and local meteorologists). Figure 9.1 illustrates relationships commonly obtained.

In some instances, the consumption curves will indicate a need for alterations. For instance, relatively high summertime consumption often results where heating boilers also provide domestic hot water; it may be better to arrange some other form of water heating and switch the boilers off. If fuel consumption is only weakly dependent on outside temperatures, then either the system is grossly undersized or ineffectively controlled, and modifications are desirable.

Whether alterations are made or not, a knowledge of the past performance of the plant allows the likely future fuel use to be predicted, using temperature or degree-day figures for average years. By comparing this with the actual monthly figures, early warning of problems may be obtained and the value of energy-saving measures may be evaluated. For instance, an increase in fuel consumption from year to year could indicate faulty or badly-maintained equipment, a loss of interest in operating the system and setting controls effectively, or increasing use of the church.

For churches in weekend use, the scanty data available suggests the following levels of annual energy consumption per cubic metre of heated volume.

5–10 kWh/m^3	The church is either underheated or makes good use of local or fast-responding heating.
10–15 kWh/m^3	This range is common for large churches with all types of heating and small churches with unit space heating.
15–20 kWh/m^3	This range is common for small churches with central heating, and churches generally, where reasonable comfort conditions are attempted with older central heating systems sized for continuous use and with insufficient capacity to permit a reasonably fast warm-up.

The figures compare with 50–100 kWh/m^3 per annum for other building types such as houses, schools and offices, and for churches in regular daily use. For a given type of system the consumption index will tend to be higher for the small church, which has a proportionately greater heat loss, and where controls are usually less sophisticated than in larger installations.

9.3. Improving Energy Efficiency

Most efforts to improve heating system efficiency and to reduce building heat loss will be successful to some degree, though more often in improving performance and comfort than necessarily in saving energy. In selecting the most cost-effective, the normal order of priority is:

1. Good management: maintaining equipment properly, reviewing standards and scheduling the use of spaces to minimise the area occupied and their heating needs, arranging for controls to be correctly set, switching equipment off when it is not needed, and carefully-considered draughtproofing to avoid excessive air infiltration (particularly in smaller churches, provided they are not damp).
2. Improving controls, particularly temperature and time controls and adding zone controls to avoid heating unused areas.
3. Altering heating systems, particularly to improve efficiency and reduce fuel cost, and adding local systems where appropriate, if necessary sub-dividing the church by means of curtains, partitions and screens.
4. Improving the insulation of the building.

In industry, Energy Managers are now appointed to monitor fuel use and to make sure that the appropriate studies are undertaken,discussions held, and recommendations implemented. Churches should consider giving one of their officers a similar task. Since energy use ultimately results from what people require and how they behave, full discussion and publicity of energy matters is essential.

The Department of Energy provides an information service and an Energy Survey Scheme where a contribution is made to the cost of a specialist energy consultant. The consultant's time is usually limited and he will do the best job if good background material on the building, its heating system, typical temperature and hours of use, and past fuel bills, is made available for him.

Church energy surveys reveal a number of recurrent causes of energy waste:

Poor operating practice. Nobody is responsible or quite understands what the system is supposed to do. Since there are usually no instructions, a rich folklore has often developed about what is best. Each fuel bill is monitored only in horror and nothing positive is done.

Poor maintenance. Often a maintenance contractor exists but he has not done a thorough job, maybe because he has not been given the funds for the necessary work. A dirty or badly-adjusted boiler can easily consume 20–30% more fuel than it ought to. Once the equipment has been cleaned and readjusted, if the efficiency is much under 70% there may be good reasons for considering replacement.

Crude controls, many systems having only an on-off switch and perhaps a high limit thermostat. Investment in better time and temperature controls, and instruction in their use, will usually be quickly repaid on all but the fastest-responding local systems (which can usefully have a timer to stop them remaining on by mistake).

Controls not effective as badly set, poorly selected, difficult to understand, badly located, and without clear instructions. More than half the time switches the author has seen in churches are either unused or not fully exploited for these reasons.

Excessive area heated, particularly where a number of spaces are on the same central system, where zone controls or local auxiliary heating should be considered.

Excessive heat output in places. Thermostats may be insufficiently accurate or have failed or been tampered with. With central heating, the church may be cold but adjacent rooms (passages, WCs, vestry) may be too warm. Thermostatic radiator valves may be added to reduce local output; settings may be secured by fitting tamperproof guards.

Hot water. Large and sometimes uninsulated tanks may be heated continuously to unnecessarily high temperatures to satisfy infrequent demands, and circulating pipes may also be kept hot. The heat may be provided very inefficiently during the summer by a central heating boiler vastly over-sized for the duty and which could otherwise be off.

Central heating system losses. Equipment in the boiler room and pipes and ducts which do not contribute usefully to space heating should be well insulated. Sluggish circulation should be improved by upgrading or adding pumps.

Low boiler efficiencies, particularly with older, oil-fired boilers. Substantial energy and money savings will often result from replacement by modern gas-fired equipment. The number and size of boilers should be reviewed at the same time. Conversion of oil boilers to gas-firing is also tempting but results may be disappointing as efficiencies sometimes drop: good technical advice should be obtained.

Undersized heat emitters, requiring needlessly long heating periods. A sound system may be extended or retained as cold weather background to a supplementary local or fast-responding system.

FIG. 9.2. DESTRATIFYING FANS

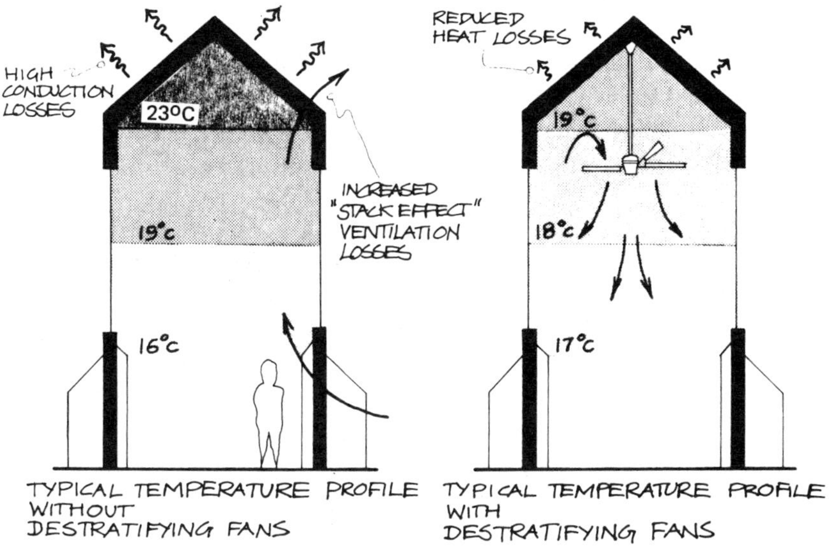

Bad stratification, where it occurs, may be counteracted by fans which blow the warm air down to low level (figure.9.2). Design and operation must ensure that the fans do not cause uncomfortable draughts which negate their effect. Some users run the fans only during the warm-up period and switch them off when the church is occupied.

Inappropriate frost protection arrangements and settings on wet central heating systems.

For more radical changes, the following points should be borne in mind:

Local heating is generally more energy-efficient than overall space heating particularly for occasional needs.

If intermittent space heating is required, radiant or unit air heating will tend to be more economical, particularly in a small church.

Operation should be very carefully considered, and controls selected and sited accordingly.

If the existing heating is in good order, it may be worth supplementing it rather than replacing it entirely.

If the fabric of the building is to be altered, the following priority list for reducing heating requirements is common:

1. Insulation over existing ceilings, detailed to avoid condensation problems. Voids should be inspected regularly for a year or two after insulation, preferably in cold weather and at times of high RH in the church, to be sure that all is well.
2. In suitable circumstances, and with due regard to acoustics, the church may be subdivided or ceilings lowered to reduce the heated volume.
3. Where the church is heated for several days at a time, insulating fills may be considered for cavity walls in good condition in sheltered locations.
4. Double glazing in unusual circumstances, e.g. to reduce bad downdraughts or to protect vulnerable stained glass windows. For stained glass external secondary glazing is often the most effective, where visually acceptable.

For churches in intermittent use, the payback periods for these measures will often be far longer than the five year maximum commonly used commercially. The work may nevertheless be justified by the long life of a church and if funds are raised by separate appeal.

Finally, however, there is no point in making the church comfortable and reducing fuel costs if the process creates conditions inimical to the building and its contents. It is best to set down the specific requirements and the things that are likely to need monitoring on a regular or occasional basis. The situation should then be reviewed formally from time to time, using instrumentation where necessary, particularly before and after making potentially significant alterations.